LIFE AFTER

Life After

by

Dr. Mohan Makkar

Ph.D. (A.M.)

Winsome Books India

ISBN: 81-88043-24-9

Edition 2004

Published by
WINSOME BOOKS INDIA
209, F-17, Harsha Complex, Subhash Chowk,
Laxmi Nagar, Delhi-110 092
Email: winsomebooks@rediffmail.com

contents

Foreword

Dear Reader,

The last decade has seen many changes in my life. As a healer, teacher of Alternate Medicines, curing thousands of cases with my students, and, teaching hundreds, I was often forced to take on cases wherein exorcism was required.

The first time I took an exorcism case, I was hit and my carotid arteries burst. I was brain dead for a few hours, my left side was paralyzed. As of today, 10% of my memory is still lost.

The next time I took an exorcism case, I had a major heart attack at night 3 a.m. Again 10% of my heart has been dead till date. But, I survived the heart attack. Angiography was done at a government hospital and my by by-pass surgery was done the following month. I regained consciousness after more than 36 hours.

What happened during those 36 hours, memories elude me, but in this haziness I can see *"an angel with wings .... flying through a door in the clouds .... Sighting Jesus, Buddha, Sai and other entities, entities playing on musical instruments .... Many of them with wings, but, covered in white cloths. Complete silence prevailed and then the sudden commanding voice, "you have to go back"... thereafter,* the light slaps on my face, I half opened my eyes and saw my doctor, he was saying "Mr. Makkar, are you all right?"

On the ninth day of my by pass surgery, I recovered completely, and, was on full time duty. All medications stopped from the second month of my leaving the hospital.

I did not give a thought to my dream ... NDE?! But, till date continue to heal, teach and of-course write.

A thought was given to me. Why not study the ***'Life & Death?'*** I did so, and present this book to you with Love and understanding. *Do not fear death, for life always begins after death.* ***"You never die"***

Love & Light

Dr. Mohan Makkar Ph.D. (A.M.)

I always play with a game with the students who are all newly introduced to me. A simple question like "Alex, are you there?"

The answer is always the same "Yes, Sir, I am here"

Aha .. the scapegoat.

"Where are you?" I ask mischievously

"Here Sir"

"Where here"

Always a puzzled look, then, "Here, here sir, in front of you." Smart Alec.

I smile, "Okay, can you touch yourself?"

"Yes, Sir" answers Alex, touching his chest.

My smile broadens, "That's your chest Alex, where are you?"

The mystery is deepening. Alex is totally confused. He touches various parts of his body, but finally gives up trying to achieve, what he now things is impossible.

Alex sits down. I look at all the other students. Take a deep breath and with dancing eyes ask softly "Can anyone here, touch themselves?"

Silence. Pin drop silence. Heads bowed down. No answer. "Okay," I pursue the subject, "let me ask you one question, if you cannot touch yourself, then where are you located?"

Silence. Then, "To know where you are, we have to go through a pattern, pattern What is Birth, The first breath, Life, Near Death Experience, Death, and Life after. Are you ready for this journey?"

A chorus "Yes Sir"

And the journey begins with this book "Life After"

- **Dear Friends,**
- **The responsibility of this book is placed on a fictional character taking birth as "Manushya"**
- **Manushya journeys through life, learning all the time.**
- **We learn along with Manushya and do as he did.**
- **Are we sincere in our learning as Manushya is?**
- **Access yourself sincerely.**
- **Love & Light**

"Manushya" is born. Today is his birthday.

A layman would ask what is a "Birth"?

According to a dictionary, "Birth" is defined as:

- *"the time when something begins" (especially life); (they divorced after the birth of the child"; "his election signaled the birth of a new age)*
- *"the event of being born"; (they celebrated the birth of their*

first child)

- *"one of the two points in child development where change is relatively sudden, in this case where the child reaches the outside world after being in the womb for nine months".*
- *Whatever the meaning, for me, it is "the instant the child comes out of the womb, the birth takes place..."*
- *Understood, the birth has taken place, but, has life taken place? How do we know that? Simply, "The first breath..."*

Manusha is now born and life has begun with 'the first breath'... That is the story on the life of MANUSHYA, which lies in between two breaths, *'the first' and the 'last breath'.*

"Manushya" is endowed with the physical anatomy; let me explain to you in short

THE PHYSICAL ANATOMY

The Vedic Reiki – The Physical Anatomy of Matter known as 'Adhibautika" teaches us for four senses in each division, now, each division is divided into five sections.

The First Sense – *'Knowledge Acquiring Senses'* – known as *'Jnana Indriyas'*. Their five sections are:

1. Ears
2. Eyes
3. Nose
4. Tongue
5. Skin.

The Second Sense – *'Working Senses'* – known as *'Karma Indriyas'*. Their five sections are:

1. Hands
2. Legs
3. System of Speech
4. Reproductive System
5. Digestive System

The Third Sense – *"Objects of the Knowledge Acquiring Senses"* – known as *"Vishayas"*. Their five sections are:

1. Sound
2. Sight
3. Smell
4. Taste
5. Touch

The Fourth Sense – *"Objectives of the Working Senses"* –

known as *"Pravritis"*. Their five sections are:

1. Holding, Pulling, Pushing
2. Walking, Running, Standing, Jumping, Kicking, Speaking, Singing
3. Sexual, Reproductive
4. Eating, Digesting and Evacuating

Taking physiology, we have talked about the senses. Now, we come to Neurology. The 'Meridians' or as we call the 'Nadis.' Remember, there are 10 Vein groups or Nadi Groups.

? The Ida and Pingala Nadis start from the right and left toes, go up gradually in a scissors pattern parallel to the back bone, into the head, and then passing through the nostrils return to the anus. (Let's keep on totaling – 2 Nadis Ida & Pingala Nadis)

? The Susumna Nadi appears at the bottom of the anus. It combines with Ida and pingala and with life air goes unto the top of head, sharing breaths. (1 Nadi – Susumna Nadi)

? The Gandhari Nadi climbs from the navel, adjusting with the seven great veins. It spreads around the throat and takes seat under the tongue. (1 Nadi – Gandhari Nadi)

? The Atti and Sikhu Nadis start from the anus and run up into the ears, protecting the instruments of hearing. (2 Nadis – Atti& Sikhu Nadis)

? The Alampurusa and Alampada Nadis start from anus, run up into the eyeballs, directing their movement. (2

Nadis – Alampurusa and Alampada Nadis)

? The Sangini and Guhu Nadis start from the navel and end under anus Ida. (2 Nadis – Sangini and Guhu Nadis)

To summarize: That's 2+1+1+2+2+2 = 10 main Nadis as above.

What is the function of these main Nadis according to Homeopathy?

? Ida, Pingala and Susumna combine in 'vata' creating constipation and other digestive problems, bringing lethargy and laziness, tamas.

? Gandhari, Atti, Sikhu and Alampurusa combine in 'pitha' creating excessive heat, thirst, gastric upheavals, pressure, and bring up lusty desires, rajas.

? Guhu, Sangini and Alampada combine in 'kapha' creating widening of the eyes, deepening of the eye-socket, excessive sweating of face, and anxiety resulting in depression, deeper tamas.

To give life to the Nadis and for our senses to work, we have been given ten kinds of "Life Airs" – known as "Pranas" divided in two categories:

Category 1 — "The vital force of life"

This includes 5 main categories of "Life air", viz.,

• Prana, • Apana, • Vyana, • Samana and • Udana,

Category 2 — "The vital force of life" is assisted by "subtle life-airs" viz.,

• Naga, Kurma, • Gregara, • Devadatta, and • Dananjaya.

The vital force is like a snake because it is sustained by air, (snakes can subsist simply by drinking air) and when there is derangement of air, the vital force is weakened and thus with lesser resistance the body becomes a victim of diseases.

Mental diseases are results of derangement of the subtle airs. Harmonizing the sustenance of vital force by meditation (like Reiki meditation) is especially beneficial to keep the airs 'in order' so that the diseases of the body become almost 'nil' by such exercise.

When this is properly done, vital force need not be used up unnecessarily in fighting diseases. Thus, naturally the life span will also increase. *If one becomes really perfect in this, even control of death is possible, as has been proved by the great yogis of India.*

FUNCTIONING OF THE VITAL LIFE FORCE:

(1) "Prana" appears

- in the 'middle of eyebrows' in the Ajna Chakra...
- then falls into the vein called 'Citra'...
- vibrates 'Aum' in the pelvis (Muladhara Chakra)...
- echoes 'Reem' in the naval (Manipuraka Chakra)...
- runs through the Ida and Pingala nadi)...
- moves around the skull...

– ...and exits through the nostrils at four to twelve finger-spaces. For a perfect body, in 24 minutes it gives 360 breathes. Per day there are 21,600 breaths – 7,200 exhalations and 14,400 inhalations.

(2) 'Apana' flows from the naval down, functioning between the anus and genitals, helping evacuation of Liquids and solids.

(3) Vyana is established in the shoulders. It works with 7,200 veins helping the limbs to fold and extend. It distributes the food nutrition equally so that bile does not increase.

(4) Udana increases the fire in belly helping digestion.

(5) Samana is established in the navel. It balances other airs, purifies the water and food intake and spreads all over the body protecting the balance.

FUNCTIONING OF THE 'SUBTLE LIFE FORCES'

(1) Naga helps one to understand arts and crafts. It also controls the functioning of sight, opening and closing of the eyelids, and the hair's standing on end.

(2) Kurma stays close to the mind, helping yawning, closing of the mouth, and laughing.

(3) Grigara helps the cleansing of the tongue and nostrils, and the functioning of coughing and sneezing.

(4) Devadatta creates laziness and anger. It flows between the anus and the genitals.

(5) Dhananjaya is seated in the nostrils. It helps the body to swell when 'prana' leaves, and cracks through the head on the third day after the death.

We know come to the "Five Vital Centers" known as "Asayas" and the locations positions in the physical body.

(1) 'Annasaya' is seated at the junction of drinking and eating.

(2) 'Jalasaya' is seated at the junction where water separates from intake of food.

(3) 'Malasaya' is seated in the junction where stool separates.

(4) 'Slanchalasaya' is seated in the junction where urine separates.

(5) 'Suklasaya' is seated in the junction where semen is stored.

The last, but, not the least "The Five Layers" known as "Koshas" and their functions:

(1) 'Annamaya' protects the gross body.

(2) 'Pranamaya' combines the working senses and the activities of the subtle body while dreaming.

(3) 'Manomaya' combines with the working senses and the functioning of the subtle body in dreams.

(4) 'Vijnanamaya' combines with the intelligence and senses and functions in dreams.

(5) 'Anandamaya' is the basis of the causal body.

Finally, there are 'Three Components' – known as 'Dhatus'

(1) 'Air' (Vayu or Vata) is produced when fire and water mix in life-air.

(2) 'Bile' (Pitha) is produced when fire and air mix in life-air.

(3) 'Mucus' (Kapha) is produced when water, fire and air mix in the life-air, separate from the body.

Now, that we know what "Manushya" is endowed with, we will see his life.

"Manushya" takes his first breath. Life has been instilled in him.

To differentiate between the wrongs & rights, the good and the bad, the SOUL is placed in him. What is this SOUL?

A lecture given by Swami Krishnananda of The Divine Life Society, Sivananda Ashram, Rishikesh, India has been given on LIFE based on The Chhandogya Upanishad.

Now we are introduced into another important aspect of this subject, namely, the stages of consciousness. You may call these the stages of the realization of the Atman, which manifests itself through the conditions known as waking, dream and deep sleep, a subject, which is elaborately discussed in the Mandukya Upanishad. Here also, it is discussed in an equally important and interesting manner by means of an anecdote, which is very famous in the Upanishads.

The anecdote:

On one occasion, Prajapati made an announcement.

"This Atman is free from every kind of evil. It is unaffected by old age or decay of any kind. It has no connection with death. It is free from mortality. Death cannot touch it. It is immortal. It is free from every kind of grief, turmoil or trouble we see in this life. It has no hunger and no thirst. These do not affect it in any manner. Its will is truthful. Its wishes are immediately materialized.

All the desires arising from here are immediately fulfilled without any limit of space or time. This Atman is to be investigated into. This Atman is to be known. Whoever investigates into this Atman and knows the nature of this Atman attains all the worlds and fulfils all desires. This is the great benefit accruing to the knower of the Atman."

It excited the curiosity of many who heard it. The gods and the demons both heard this proclamation made in that celestial assembly.

The gods hurried back to their homes and held a conference among themselves with Indra as their chief. They said,

"Brahma has told us such an interesting thing! Whoever knows the Atman has mastery over all the worlds and has the capacity to fulfill every wish or desire. We must know this Atman. Some of us should be deputed for getting training in the school of Brahma. We must get initiated into this mystery of the Atman."

The gods chose Indra, their chief, as the proper deputy and sent him to Brahma. They said to him, "Go and have training under Brahma and know this Atman, because he has already made an announcement, that if we know it, such wonderful results would follow."

Similar was the reaction of the asuras, the demons. They also heard this. They went back to their world and then held a conference. They said, "This Atman is a very wonderful thing and we must know this Atman." So they deputed their chief, Virochana, for the purpose. They told him, "You go to Brahma and have training in this wisdom of the Atman, so that we too will be benefited by this knowledge as was proclaimed." This was the outcome of this announcement.

Both went to Brahma's place and approached him as humble disciples with the sacred offering of samit. And having gone there, it does not appear that they said anything. From what the Upanishad says, it appears that they stayed there for thirty-two years without saying anything, observing austerity, controlling their senses and living a very disciplined life. They lived in the abode of Brahma, having said nothing either between themselves or to Brahma himself.

Then after thirty-two years of this kind of living there, Brahma seems to have observed their stay and asked them: *"What is the matter with you? Why are you staying here for so many years observing self-discipline? What do you want?"* Then both of them said the same thing, *"We are here for some purpose."* *"What is that purpose?"* queried Prajapati. They replied, *"O*

Great Lord, we have heard your great proclamation. You made an announcement that the knower of the Atman fulfils all desires, has mastery over all the worlds and is unaffected by pains of any kind. In search of the knowledge of the Atman have we come here. This is the purpose of our visit, and for this reason it is that we have been living here for thirty-two years observing austerity." "Oh, that is very good," said Prajapati.

And inasmuch as they had already undergone some discipline, Brahma did not ask them to undergo any further vow or any other formality. He immediately started giving initiation: *"You want to know the Atman? Here is this knowledge."* He gave a very pithy and precise instruction, which could be, interpreted this way or that way.

"That Being which you see in your eye is the Atman,"

said Prajapati. It was a very strange statement indeed. This was all the instruction. There was no further explanation whatsoever. He is right in what he said, but it can be very easily misconstrued. *"That* ***Purusha,*** *the being that you see in your eyes, that is the Atman. Are you satisfied? I have given you an initiation. This is the immortal, this is the abode of fearlessness, this is the Absolute."*

Immediately the whole instruction was misconstrued by both the disciples, just as any one of us would have done. They at once came to the same conclusion regarding the reflection seen in the eye. We know what is seen in the eye. A body is reflected. What can be reflected in the eye except a body? *"Oh, I see, this is the Atman. What is reflected in the eye is the Atman"* — thus concluded both Indra and Virochana. *"Then, what is reflected in water, is that the Atman?"* they asked.

"That which is reflected in the mirror, is that also Atman?" They were so happy that the Atman is so easy to reach. So they want to get this instruction confirmed by asking, *"Which is the Atman, that is seen as reflected in the water or that seen as reflected in the mirror? Is that also the Atman? Is it true? Is it so?"* They queried Brahma, and his answer was very simple. He said, *"It is seen in every kind of reflection." "Well, is it in the water?"* they again asked. *"Yes, in water also. It is reflected everywhere,"* he replied.

A very short instruction! And both were very happy. The disciples felt that they had known the Atman. Actually the teacher must have felt pity for the ignorance of these disciples who immediately misunderstood the whole teaching and thought the physical body could be the Atman, because that alone can be reflected in this manner. What else can be reflected if not an external object!

The Bodily Self

Now Brahma said, *"Please go and look at yourselves in a pan of water and see what is there; if you cannot understand anything about the Atman, then let me know."* They went and saw themselves in a pan of water. Then Brahma asked them, *"What do you see?"* They immediately gave the answer: *"Up to the hair and the nails, everything that we are, we see exactly reflected in this water. This is what we see. We see ourselves as we are."*

Then Brahma said, *"This is the Atman."* Now what Brahma said was highly significant. But the mystery behind the instruction was so deep that the disciples again grossly misunderstood it. Whatever we see is God — this is generally what we say. It is a true statement, no doubt. But it is also an untrue statement. The untrue aspect of it can simply take us astray. But the true aspect of it will, of course, liberate us from bondage. So is the instruction of Brahma. *"What you see in your eyes is the Atman. What you see in the reflection is the Atman. This is the Atman, this is the fearless abode, this is the Absolute."*

So they were told about what they saw as their reflection. Happy and composed in heart, both the students went back thinking that they have known the Atman.

When they had gone out of sight, Prajapati thought, "What a pity! These students have understood nothing from me. They have mistaken my teaching completely. They are thinking that their own body is the Atman, and if any one is to consider this body as the Atman and regard it as the ultimate Reality, and teach others a doctrine that this material body is the Atman, it will not succeed. Those who follow this doctrine are going to be defeated everywhere."

Virochana went to the demons and said, *"I have received initiation. Now I know what the Atman is, by which you can control all the worlds and fulfill all your desires. This body itself, what we see here, is the Atman. This is what Prajapati told us. This body is to be adorned beautifully and taken care of well. It is to be tended well, because it is the Reality. There is nothing more real than this body. It is to be protected by any manner available. It is the knowledge of this Reality, this Atman, and this physical embodiment that will help us in fulfilling all our desires. The body is an instrument for the fulfillment of desires and it is through the instrumentality of this body that you have to control all the worlds."* This is the doctrine of the crass materialist and the sensualist that the demons learnt from Virochana. This became the doctrine of the **asuras.**

To this day people generally say, *"Here is a demon"* when a person has no charitable nature. He who has no faith in the super-physical realms, who never worships deities above this world, who never performs sacrifices of any kind, who is intensely selfish, self-centred and body-centred, is generally.

This demoniacal doctrine was proclaimed as a consequence of the initiation that Virochana received from Brahma in respect of the Atman. This is the fate of Virochana and his followers.

Now what happened to Indra? Did he also follow the same doctrine? Poor man! He did not reach home at all. Halfway itself he had doubts in the mind. He thought, "How could this body be the Atman? That cannot be, because if what is reflected in water or reflected anywhere, which is nothing but this body, is the Atman, then the Atman would be affected by every kind of defect to which the body is subject. So there would be a defective Atman. This Atman cannot then be called immortal. This body is subject to death. When this body goes, the Atman also will go, if the body is the Atman. Where then come fearlessness and immortality and ***brahmatva*** mentioned by the Creator? There seems to be some mistake in my understanding of this teaching." So he had these doubts and he did not go to the gods to communicate this knowledge. Instead, he returned immediately to Prajapati.

Indra had great sorrow and fear in his heart. He thought within himself, "If I am well-dressed, the Atman is also well-dressed. If the body is blind, the Atman is blind. If the body is crippled, the Atman also is crippled. Finally when the body dies, the Atman also will die. Well, this follows as a consequence of taking this body as the Atman. So it is a destructible Atman into which I have been initiated? This is no good. I shall go back to the great master once again and clarify this position."

Again with humble offering, Indra went to Brahma with discomfiture and doubts. His doubts were that the Atman cannot be the visible body or anything visible whatsoever because everything that is visible is physical in nature and is characterized by the defects of everything that is physical. Prajapati questioned Indra regarding his doubts. *"You went satisfied, and now what makes you come back?" "Great master,"* replied Indra, *"how can we regard this body as the Atman when it is subject to these defects?*

If this body is blind, the Atman will become blind. If the body is diseased, the Atman would have disease. If the body dies, the Atman will die! So what kind of Atman is this? For these reasons, the reflection cannot be the Atman.

"I have great doubts. I have come to you for clarification.

Perhaps I have misconstrued your teaching. I am having knowledge of a perishable Atman. What is the truth about this matter? Please initiate me further."

"Well, I shall speak to you again, but live here a life of austerity for another thirty-two years. Afterwards I shall speak to you," said Brahma.

Thirty-two years had already passed and again another thirty-two years had to be lived with Prajapati under severe discipline, self-control and aspiration. After the second thirty-two years of disciplined life at the abode of Prajapati, Indra was given fresh instructions.

"What is reflected in the eye or reflected in the water may not be the Atman for the reason you have already mentioned," said Prajapati. *"Now I introduce you into a greater reality which is unaffected by the conditions of the physical body. That has to be regarded as the Atman because if the doubt is that the Atman about which instruction has been received is affected by physical character, then naturally that which is not so affected should be regarded as the Atman."*

The Dream Self

Prajapati now said, *"That which you see in the state of dream is the Atman. That is Brahman about which I am going to speak to you. That Being which rejoices and is happy in the state of dream is the Atman, which is fearless and which is immortal. This is the Reality about which I have spoken earlier and into which you seek initiation."*

Well, to some extent there was satisfaction of Indra's doubts. The physical body does not affect the conditions in dream. *"Yes, this must be so,"* he thought, and went back, cool, calm and composed in heart. But he was blessed with the capacity to ratiocinate and investigate into what he was told. On the way, before he reached his palace in heaven, he again had a doubt.

"How, could this be?" he thought within himself. *"That which is in dream is the Atman? Can it be like that? Yes, if the body is blind, the dream person need not be blind. And if the bodily individual has any other defect such as crippleness, etc., this defect does not affect the dreaming individual. Perhaps even if the physical body is amputated, a limb cut off or affected very seriously, the dreaming individual is not so affected."*

Now Indra had another doubt. Even if it be that the dreamer is not affected by the defects of the physical body, there is some other defect in dream. One is not always perfect in dream. The point whether the physical body affected the dream body or not is irrelevant. What is pertinent here is that the dreaming individual has the same problems as the waking individual. There is the same pleasure and pain dependent on unreliable factors both in the waking and dreaming body. One feels as if one is chased or driven away or being killed even in dream. One feels sorrow and grief and passes through unpleasant experiences in dream also. Can this then be the Atman? Naturally, it cannot be, because it is not perfect. It is affected by the same changes, which the waking body is subjected to. One cries, weeps and sobs when one has painful experiences in dream also. This dreaming Atman is no good. This was the trend of thought which Indra had in his mind when he was halfway to his city in the heavens.

Again with sacred firewood, Indra approached Prajapati as a humble disciple. Prajapati queried, *"This is the third time. You went away satisfied, O Indra. Now again you have come. What is wrong?"*

Indra mentioned once again all his doubts. *"This dreaming individual is no good at all,"* said he. *"The dreaming person can be sorry, can be affected in a serious manner like the waking one and he has even the experience of destruction, death, etc. What is the good of this Atman? This is my doubt. Please teach me the real Atman."*

"Another thirty-two years you stay here, leading a life of discipline. Let me see then if I can tell you something more about the Atman," said Prajapati. This is the third time that he was asked to live a life of self-control. Indra must have been a tenacious person, no doubt, to stay like this for the sake of the great knowledge which he sought, by the acquisition of which he aspired for mastery over all the worlds and fulfillment of every kind of desire.

So he, according to the injunction of Prajapati, stayed there, the latter's abode, for another thirty-two years, leading a life of intense discipline, austerity and ***tapascharya***. After these thirty-two years, Prajapati instructed Indra again.

"Now, I will tell you something different. I will point out the Atman which is not affected by the physical body, nor conditioned by the sorrows of dream, and which is blessed in its own state.

What is that? He who is in the deep sleep state that is the Atman. This is the immortal, this is the fearless, this is the Atman. Which one? That which is in the state of deep sleep," said Prajapati.

Now, that which is in the state of deep sleep has no experience of sorrow of any kind. It does not feel that it is affected by anything. It has no grief. It does not feel that it dies. So in a sense it is all right. The sleeping state is a state of freedom from all the turmoils of both the physical and psychic life in the waking and the dreaming states.

Listening to these instructions of Prajapati, Indra was satisfied for the time being. So, he left Prajapati's abode and went back home thinking that he had known the Atman. But, on the way he again had doubts. He did not reach home. He had great fear.

"What sort of Atman is this that is in sleep? It is as if it is not there at all! It is a zero, annihilation, and a negation of all things! This Atman is a darkness, which knows neither its own self nor others. What kind of thing is this sleep? Neither it knows that it is, nor does it know that anything else is. It is like complete annihilation, as it were. How could self-annihilation be the Atman? This kind of Atman is no good. That which does not know its own Self! What sort of Atman is this?" With these doubts, Indra again went back to Prajapati.

With sacred fuel in hand, Indra came to Prajapati as a disciple once again to learn the truth about the Atman. Prajapati asked, *"O Indra, why have you come back again? You went away satisfied after receiving my instruction."* Indra replied, *"This Atman in deep sleep that you spoke to me about does not know anything at all. It is an ignorant Atman. This is a state of apparent self-annihilation. I cannot believe that this is the immortal Atman, by knowing which one becomes the lord of all the worlds and fulfils all desires, and about which you made a proclamation in your court. Kindly teach me about that Atman."*

"Another five years of discipline is necessary. So stay here for another five years," said Prajapati. According to the advice of the great master, he lived there again for five years with intense discipline, and sought initiation again. So, one hundred and one years of *tapas* did Indra perform in the abode of Prajapati for the sake of this Supreme Knowledge. Even now people say: *"Indra, such a powerful person with such a brilliant intellect, had to live a life of tremendous austerity for one hundred and one years for the sake of this Atman knowledge!"*

What to speak of other ordinary people! How much discipline is necessary! How much preparation is called for! And what intense austerity has to precede this seeking of knowledge from a teacher! This shows the need for the requisite preparation for the reception of this knowledge. It cannot come easily. After these preparations on the part of Indra and his having completed one hundred and one years of tremendous *tapas*, Prajapati instructed about the final truth about the Atman.

THE DISCOURSE ON WHAT 'ATMA' 'SOUL' IS :

Prajapati said: *"This is the great truth, O Indra. This is the Atman. Now do you understand what the Atman is? This is the Supreme Person, if you would call IT a person."* It is not a person actually. We call it a person only by way of expression, explanation for the purpose of helping the understanding of the immature mind. It is the Supreme Being. That is how we translate the term *Uttama-purusha,* occurring here. Superior to the transitory *purushas,* we have the universal *Purusha*. The word *Uttama-purusha* occurs in the Bhagavad-Gita also in its fifteenth chapter, where we are told that there are two *purushas,* the *kshara* and the *akshara,* and that there is the third, the supreme one, the *Purushottama* or the *Uttama-purusha,* which means to say that there is something transcending both the perishable universe and the imperishable, immanent consciousness.

These descriptions pertain to the life of spiritual freedom, sometimes called *Jivanmukti.* In the usual language of the Vedanta philosophy, there is that state known as *Jivanmukti* which means spiritual Liberation even when the body is there apparently.

There are umpteen descriptions of what *Jivanmukti* is, and there is limitation in all these descriptions. It is held by people that the so-called existence of the body of the *Jivanmukta* is there from the point of view of others who see him and not from his own point of view. This is one way of looking at it. We cannot say whether he himself is aware of the body or not. But others see it.

So, as long as others see the existence and the movement of the body of that individual, that individual is supposed to be a *Mukta* with a body. That is why he is called *Jivanmukta.*

Others are of opinion that he may also be aware of his own physical existence in a different way altogether from what we feel in respect of our own bodies.

The consciousness of the existence of the body is not necessarily an evil, provided it is experienced in the proper perspective. It is the ignorance that is the cause of bondage and not merely the existence of this thing or that thing. The mere presence of the body will not be a bondage provided it is known in its reality.

This again is a very difficult thing to grasp. What is it to know a thing in reality? No one can explain these things unless one goes to this state personally. And no one can understand it also unless one enters this state. It is usually held that one experiences in this condition of *Jivanmukti* a tremendous freedom of attainment and achievement.

That sort of freedom is it? It is not a freedom to do anything that one likes in the sense of a license given to an immature individual. It is a freedom that comes, on account of a knowledge of the depths of everything, not only a knowledge in the sense of an ordinary accumulation of facts by logical knowledge, but an insight into the nature of Reality by identity of being.

To understand as to what the behaviour of this person would be in respect of others, we have only to imagine for the time being what would be our attitude towards a thing in respect of which we have established identity of existence.

It is well nigh impossible to conceive it, as long as we have not experienced it, but by a stretch of imagination we can, to some extent, feel what that state could be. How do we feel in respect of the thing with which we are one? What is our attitude towards it? Well, it is neither one of attachment nor one of repulsion, neither one of like nor one of dislike, but a feeling of complete mastery over it. This is the characterization of that state where one is in identity with everything and yet is not attached to anything or repulsed by anything.

The freedom that one experiences in the state of *Jivanmukti* is, therefore, one of complete mastery born of identity of being, and not a mastery in the sense of control of one person by another person as we see in this world. It is not the exercise of power by one person in respect of another. It is an exuberance of the abundance of power, which is inseparable from the universality of Being.

Ultimately power is one with Being itself. So, this is something very enigmatic, very difficult to grasp ordinarily. It is nothing but the difficulty in explaining God himself. It is God-being that we are describing when we speak of *Jivanmukti,* an embodiment so called which becomes the vehicle of God-experience in this world itself. Such is *Jivanmukti* about which Prajapati is speaking in these passages.

The perception of a *Jivanmukta* is now described very precisely in one or two sentences. With our present state of mind it is not possible to understand what the perception of *Jivanmukta* could be. We can only have comparisons, illustrations and analogies. But what actually it is, it is not possible for us to understand. Some of us may be under the impression that he sees God, and does not see the world. This is the usual way of giving an opinion about the experiences of a *Jivanmukta.* As I have already stated, these are all our ways of looking at things and our ways of thinking.

There is no such thing as seeing God and not seeing the world. Such differences, such contrasts do not find a place in a vision, which sees what Truth is. There is a lot of controversy among the different schools of thought as to whether the world is seen by the *Jivanmukta* or not. It all depends upon what is meant by the word 'world'. He sees the world! Yes. Or he does not see the world. Both statements are correct. He sees the world as it really is, and he does not see the world as it appears to the senses which are distorted in their structure. Our relative values should not be carried to this realm of universal perfection. It would be unbecoming on our part to appraise the experiences of.

There is no world even now and the question of seeing the world, or not seeing the world, does not actually arise. Whatever is there now, will be there even afterwards. Just because someone has changed his mind, the world is not going to be different. But his mind has undergone discipline to such an extent, and has changed and transformed in itself, that it will see the world in the way it has to be seen.

The Upanishads are never tired of telling us that the correct way of perception is to perceive the Self in things and not to see the form in them. This is exactly what the *Jivanmukta* sees. To see the Self in a thing is not to see the thing or the object as such. Even these analogies are inadequate. We cannot understand as to what it is to see the Self in a thing.

Again we will be interpreting the Self as something outside us, to be seen with the eye of spiritual perception. It is nothing of the kind. With this cautious background we have to try to understand these very short portrayals of the grandeur of the *Jivanmuktas* given in these passages of the Upanishad. He may do exactly what you do and what I do. There is no difference in his conduct. He may speak the same language and he may eat the same food. Yet, he is not eating and he is not speaking. This is a difficult thing to understand, because these particular activities and particular modes of experience are generalized and universalized in his case, so that they no longer become obstacles to his unique experience.

They become obstacles only when they are wrested out of their universal context and made one's own, my own, your own, or made to stand on its own legs, independently of others. His actions are not individual actions, but universal movements. And he does not think as I think or you think. His is just a thought, which includes every thought. It is the general substance of every kind of mind and thought. So when the Upanishad says that he speaks, he laughs, he moves about and he enjoys, it does so from our point of view only.

The question of enjoying or speaking or moving about does

not arise for that which has no particularized consciousness, either of space, time, or movement. In the vision of other people, he will be practically speaking just like anyone else. You cannot identify a *Jivanmukta* by observing him. He will look like yourself only. But there will be a tremendous difference inside.

The electrons are not seen with our naked eyes, but the microscope can see them. You keep a solid object in front of you and gaze at the solid object, and keep also a very powerful microscope. Your eyes are seeing the object and the microscope is also is seeing the object. But the two instruments are seeing two different things altogether.

What your eyes see the microscope does not see, and what the microscope sees your eyes do not see. But, both are seeing the same thing simultaneously. Now, you are the person to judge whether the object is what your eyes see, or whether it is what the microscope sees. Which is the correct thing? This is just an example.

You see a world and the *Jivanmukta* also sees it, but he sees it differently from what you see it because of the difference of the instrument of perception. For him an instrument does not exist. He himself is the instrument and he himself is the object seen. He has become that which he is seeing and so it cannot be called seeing, but it is rather 'being'. Seeing, he does not see. It appears that he does not see, because there is nothing outside him, and yet, he sees everything because he is himself that. He cannot be conscious of the body. He is not only in one body. He is in every body.

Whatever you think is his thought and whatever anybody thinks also is his thought only. So you cannot say whether he thinks, or I think, or you think.

The consciousness of a particular body or object does not arise because all the bodies or objects are his, nay he himself. So the Upanishad says that he has no awareness of a particular encasement in some individual body. Just as bulls may be yoked to drag a cart, this Supreme Self manifests itself as the *prana* and is yoked to this cart of the body, as it were. The bulls do not become one with the cart. They are different. Likewise, this *prana* or consciousness that is yoked to the body is not identical with the body. Whatever the eyes see when they are cast into space is something different in the case of this liberated soul from what our eyes see. From the point of view of the liberated soul, when the eyes perceive something outside, it is not the eyes that are seeing the object, but it is 'something else' that sees.

This was the subtle point which was in the mind of Prajapati when he told Virochana and Indra at the very outset that whatever is reflected in the eye is the Atman. So he is right from his side. But both Indra and Virochana could not understand what his intention was. What sees through the eye is not the eye, but is something different from the eyes. And what hears through the ears too is not the ear but there is something else inside which hears through the ears. So is the case with every other sense organ. The senses do not contact the object. He who contacts is 'somebody else' utilising these senses as instruments.

This eye is only an instrument of perception. What sees an

object is not the eye. What sees through the eye is the same thing as that which hears through the ear. The eye cannot hear and the ear cannot see, and so are the functions of the other senses limited to their respective domains. There is a distinction among the functions of the different senses. But we know very well that we can integrate these perceptions through all the senses into a single whole, so that one individual being is aware simultaneously that there is seeing, hearing, etc. In our case, it is only an inference, but in the case of the liberated soul, it is an actual revelation.

It is not merely that. It is something deeper than this implication. What sees through the eye also is different from the eye, and what is seen through the eye also is different from the object. It is not the eye that sees, and it is not the object that is seen. It is 'something else' that is seen and it is the same 'something else' that sees. Therefore, the seen and the seer are one. It is as if that 'something else' is beholding itself. It is the Atman that smells, not the nose. The nose or the instrument of smelling is only a vehicle utilized by consciousness for this purpose. One that speaks is not the tongue. It is the Atman that speaks utilizing the instrument of the tongue as merely an occasion for its manifestation in that particular manner. So is the case with the ear.

The ear is only an occasion for the manifestation of the Atman. The Atman is a single, non-dual, all-pervading Being which works in these diverse ways in the forms of the senses, sense perception, and the objects of perception. So, there is really no such things as sense perceptions, the senses and their objects. It is the Atman projecting itself in every nook and corner of the universe through these orifices called the senses and contacting its own universal body, outside which we wrongly call the objects of sense. This is the truth. The liberated soul is fully aware of this truth, while others are ignorant about it, although it is the same in their case also.

Whatever thinks through the mind also is the Atman. The so-called mind is only a cognitive instrument. But it is a superior kind of instrument. It is a celestial eye provided to us. In fact, the mind alone works in *Brahma-loka.* The senses do not exist there. These manifestations in five ways as hearing, touching, seeing, tasting and smelling do not come into operation in *Brahma-loka.* The great souls living in *Brahma-loka* do not see with the eyes, do not speak with the tongue and do not eat and drink as we do. They merely exist in their mental body. There are some who even think that the mind also does not work there in the ordinary way.

It is something super-physical and non-material that becomes the vehicle for the experience of the soul in *Brahma-loka.* This celestial eye comprehends all things at one stroke, unlike the senses, which perceive only one thing at a time. This is the instrument that is used in *Brahma-loka.* The moment such a mind thinks, the whole conglomeration of objects connected with that thought appears at one stroke there in its presence. The archetypes of things are perhaps visualised in *Brahma-loka,* not the reflections.

The objects, which we see in this world, are not the originals. They are only reflections. All the originals including those of myself and yourself are in *Brahma-loka.* We are all reflections of the original. We are all unreal bodies, apparitions in some respect, looking like very important persons. Our importance is somewhere else and we are rooted in a higher realm. And we are even now connected with that realm. Our legs are there though we appear to be moving here! We are reflections and therefore distorted. We are partial and finite, on account of which we are incapable of fulfilling our desires. The original which is the whole, the infinite, alone can work. Reflections cannot really work as efficiently as the original. This efficiency in working comes only when we reach *Brahma-loka.*

Now this *Brahma-loka* does not mean some other world which is several million miles away. It is a state of consciousness. It is within these very walls of our room. It is only a higher frequency of consciousness that is called *Brahma-loka,* into which one can raise oneself even here. Really there is no question of 'here' and 'there'. These are only inappropriate terms used in connection with sense experiences for want of better terms. There is neither 'here' nor 'there', neither 'then' nor 'now'. All these words cannot apply in *Brahma-loka.* Wherever you are, there is *Brahma-loka,* if only you can tune up your mind to the high frequency of its level of consciousness.

The great gods, having Indra as their leader who obtained this superior initiation from Prajapati in the manner mentioned here, contemplate on this Atman. Therefore they are able to fulfill all their wishes by mere thought. They establish contact with their inner mind in respect of everything that they think at any moment of time. All the worlds are comprehended by them. They can penetrate throughout the universe.

Objects like huge mountains cannot impede their movement. Physical bodies are no obstacles for them. We sometimes hear in scriptures that angels fly and that gods easily move from plane to plane. This is so because they are in their subtle mental bodies. They are not physical vehicles, so they are not controlled by the power of the gravitation of the earth.

Everything is under their sway. They can have entry into every realm. They can move anywhere. All desires of theirs are fulfilled on account of this permeating consciousness which is not capable of being obstructed by anything.

This is a glorification of the knowledge of the Atman in respect of the gods who had it through Indra. This is a knowledge which can be had not only by gods alone, but anyone, including yourself and myself. It is not a prerogative of any particular person or individual. Everyone is heir-apparent to this great knowledge, provided the necessary discipline is undergone. We can imagine what hardship Indra had to pass through. Perhaps our hardship will be much more. We must be prepared to pay the price of this knowledge. Then it shall come. It can be the property of everyone, but first one has to be ready to become a receptacle for it. As is the case with all those who have realized the Self, so will be the case with everyone who attains this Knowledge. There will be complete control over things and fulfillment of everything, even of a mere wish that arises in the mind, at that very moment it arises. This is what Prajapati said in conclusion.

So, we have here an analysis of the various states of consciousness, through this story of instruction to Indra by

Prajapati. This analysis is actually the logical approach by way of inference to the existence of a consciousness deep within every one of us. What Prajapati actually wanted to drive home to the mind of the disciple was that the Atman is ubiquitously present everywhere in all the three states. That is why he said first that It is in the eye in the waking state, then in the dream state, then in the sleeping condition, and finally as something transcendent. Now, all these definitions are correct, though we should not take them literally.

The implication or the actual intention behind the instruction has to be understood. The Atman is in deep sleep state. Yes, it is true. It is in dream. It is also in waking. It is reflected through the eyes and the senses. All these statements are correct, because without the operation in some way or the other of this consciousness, there would be neither sleep, nor dream nor waking. A compartment or a wall, as it were, has been introduced by us between these various experiences, so that we are unable to connect the deeper implications of these different experiences.

When we are in one condition, we completely forget the other conditions. When we are awake, we cannot be dreaming or in deep sleep.

When we dream, we cannot be in deep sleep or awake. When we are in deep sleep, we cannot be awake or dreaming. This is our difficulty, in spite of the fact that our consciousness is one with the same substratum that is responsible for all these experiences. The difference arises on account of a peculiar faculty in us called the mind. It is not the defect of consciousness which is the same that is in me, in you, and in the *Jivanmukta*.

The so-called mind is also not an independent thing absolutely different from the Atman. It is a hybrid, as it were, born from one side partially and belonging to another side partially. However, for all practical purposes of analysis, we may say that it is the same consciousness that we call the Atman which has somehow got twisted, as it were, and focused in a single particular direction and got obsessed with the view that that direction alone is real and that every other direction is unreal and does not exist.

This obsessed movement of consciousness, the mind, in respect of a particular direction is what we call its target or the object of sense. This is a creation of its own, due to its *prarabdha* and we cannot say how and why it works. But the background is the Atman, the Consciousness. It does not vary. The mind in waking, the mind in dream, the mind in sleep and the mind that has transcended itself,all these are basically pervaded through and through, warp and woof, by the same consciousness.

The feeling that 'I exist' is the Atman speaking in its own language. This feeling is persisting even in dream, and you cannot say that it does not exist even in deep sleep. So it is there always. Not only that, It exists as self-sufficient awareness. We are aware in one way in the waking state and we are aware in a different way altogether in the other two states.

There is a difference in the structure of the awareness, because of the difference in the nature of the objects with which this particular compartment-like consciousness is connected. So we get shifted wholly due to our affiliation with the mind to these realms in which it moves, and then it is that we are unable to connect the one phase of consciousness with another phase.

So, Prajapati's instruction is a universal instruction that the Atman is present in every state. Even in the so-called unconscious state, it is there. The unconsciousness is not of the Atman. It is of the mind. It is a kind of stifling taking place in the finitude of individuality.

The finalizing principle we call the mind, and that gets suffocated, as it were. It closes its eyes in sleep, in coma, and even in death in a state of unconsciousness which cannot be attributed to the Atman. So, this is the difficulty with us.

Now the transcendent state which the great master Prajapati speaks of as bodiless, free from embodiment, is capable of being attained by means of certain disciplines as is pointed out by the Upanishad. But we are not told as to what these disciplines are. We have been told of *brahmacharya,* but we cannot fully understand what it means. Thirty-two years, again thirty-two years, a third time thirty-two years and again five years, thus one hundred and one yearsit may even be a thousand years. But what was it that Indra did all these years? Was he merely having his breakfast and lunch in the hotel of Brahma and getting on there? It was not like that. There must have been something very strange in the way of life he lived there, an inkling of which we can get from a study of the way in which students lived in ancient times in their masters' hermitages and conducted themselves wholly and solely for the purpose of the realization of the Self.

There should be a complete canalization of our aspiration in the correct direction. It is for this that we come to the masters. There should be no distraction of aim or purpose. The discipline that is spoken of in the Upanishad is nothing but a canalization of consciousness. We may call it *brahmacharya,* or we may call it self-control. It is concentration of our entire being in a given direction, so that it does not move in any other way or direction. It is like an arrow moving towards its target. The arrow will not be aware of anything else, either this way or that way. This arrow-consciousness is what is expected of us and we should not budge until the goal is reached. We are told of this sort of attitude of mind even in the case of comparatively recent personalities like Buddha and others who budged not from the aim which was given to their minds from their own point of view.

Modern times are perhaps unfit for these strict disciplines. We have umpteen problems. But the wisdom lies not in merely saying that there are problems. There were problems even for those people. We should find ourselves in the proper place. We should not misplace ourselves in unsuited contexts. We have to rise from the level in which we are, whatever the level be. It may be a child's level, an adult's level, or a mature mind's level. It may be an official's level, a student's level, or a professor's level. Each one should be able to judge for himself where he stands. He must understand what is the context in which he is placed in the background of the aspiration, what he entertains in his mind, and what are his problems.

We are told that the great Ramatirtha had a peculiar technique of his own for self-control. He used to make a list of all his desires.

It was no joke. It was an honest investigation into his own mind. To some extent we can know what our desires are. Go to a secluded place, or sit in your own room, or sit behind a temple or in a forest and think what your desires are. You should not say, "I have no desires." Nor can you say, "I do not know anything." You do know something, because it is the persistent thoughts in the mind that are your desires. When you are free from the distractions of the daily functions of life, your real desires will manifest themselves.

These desires have to be dealt with in a proper manner. That is the discipline called for. The discipline or *brahmacharya* which the Upanishad speaks of is the discipline of dealing with the desires. What are you going to do with your desires? Are you going to just swallow them, or oppose them and crush them, or fulfill them? You cannot answer this question easily. This is the reason why a superior person's guidance is necessary. These desires are like snakes. You cannot touch them, and you cannot keep them lying in a corner. You cannot do anything with them. But you cannot keep quiet also. You know very well the nature of the snakes. So a very dexterous method has to be employed.

Neither subjugating, nor crushing, nor fulfilling, in the literal sense, but tackling them in the manner they should be tackled, under the circumstances in which you are placed, considering the strength and weakness of your mind, and the consequences also of your actionsthis is the discipline. So, many factors have to be considered. All this an individual cannot do alone. Therefore, a Guru is necessary.

We are now about to enter into the realm of *Brahma.* The aspiration has gone to its zenith. So the soul speaks to itself, as it were. "I shall reach that Supreme." Literally translated the first portion of this *mantra* means, "From the dark blue one I go to the more defined one, and from the more defined one I go to the dark blue." Nobody can understand what these words mean if they are interpreted grammatically.

The commentators say that these words refer to the state of Supreme Experience. Various commentators have different meanings to say. "From the cause I go to the subtle and from the subtle I go to the cause"this is one meaning. Another meaning given is, "From Isvara I go to Hiranyagarbha and from Hiranyagarbha I go to Isvara." A third meaning given is, "From Brahman I go to Isvara and from Isvara I go to Brahman." "From the Universal I go to the Cause thereof, and from the Cause I go to the Universal," is still another interpretation. All these are exclamations of joy of the soul that is about to enter into the ocean of Being.

And how does it go to this tremendous experience? It shakes its body and cleans it up as a horse does by shaking its body and throwing off all the dust from its hairs. This is not the literal shaking off of our physical body, but a shaking off of the entire vestures of the personality. *Annamaya, pranamaya, manomaya, vijnanamaya* and *anandamaya*the physical, the vital, the mental, the intellectual and the causalall these sheaths or bodies are shed automatically.

The soul now exclaims: "I shall free myself, as the moon frees itself from the darkness of the eclipse, from the mouth of Rahu. I shall be freed from the clutches of ignorance, this darkness that has been overshadowing me up to this time. I shall shake off this body which is actually not there. I have been misled into the feeling that all along it has been there. I shall free myself from this obsession. I shall become a *kritatma,* one who has fulfilled one's purposes. The aim of life has been attained and all my purposes have been fulfilled. There is nothing left to be done now, because that which is the ultimate purpose of all my efforts and endeavors in life has been reached. I shall attain *Brahma-loka,* the Supreme Abode of the Creator. I shall reach this Abode and become one with this Abode."

Comparatively later mystics also have spoken about experiences of this kind. The great saints of India like Sant Ramdas, Tukaram, Jnanesvar Maharaj, and in the West, mystics like Plotinus have explained this experience without using the word *Brahma-loka.*

In this supernal experience, there is the consciousness of the interpenetration of things. In the words of Plotinus, everything is mirrored in everything else. It is as if everywhere we have got only mirrors to which individuals are compared. These are not physical mirrors, of course, kept in space, but non-located super-physical mirrors, if at all you can call them such, where every individual is reflected in every other individual. Everything is everywhere. This is the experience of interpenetration in *Brahma-loka.*

The space that we see here is the cause of the differentiation of name and form. What we call the objects of sense are nothing but names and forms. They manifest on account of the presence of space and time. But what is inside space and subtler than it? And is that the Absolute? We can see space but we cannot see what is beyond space, inside space. That which is internal to even the subtlest object of perception which is space is the Atman. That is Brahman, the Absolute. This is the Immortal.

Now, there is the exclamation of the liberated soul. "This is the Atman, this is Brahman. For the sake of this realization I enter the hall, the abode of Prajapati, the Creator."

In some Upanishads, like the Kaushitaki, we have very beautiful descriptions wherein are given realistic explanations of what things are met on the way by the soul in its ascent to *Brahma-loka.*

The soul enters the hall of Brahma, goes to the abode of Prajapati, the Creator, and becomes the glory of every one. Your glory and my glory, all glories are one, because the 'I' enters into everyone. Whatever is the greatness of anything, that becomes 'my' greatness. Great men, geniuses, masters, scientists, artists, whoever they be, whatever greatness they have, that is 'my' greatness, because 'I' enters into their Being, 'I' gets united with their Being. And whatever they are, that 'I' myself am. That is 'my' glory. The 'I' attains everything. 'I' am the Glory of all glories. What is the Glory of the glorious people in the world? That glory has come not from them, but from something else, and that am 'I'.

"May I not enter into this womb of the mother once again," is the last prayer of the liberated soul. He shall not enter into the womb of the mother. These peculiar words mean, "May I not enter into the womb of the mother which swallows all souls into their embodiment and limits them into personalities."

This is the great wisdom of the Chhandogya Upanishad in its quintessence.

Manushya can now enter the world. But, he does not have the knowledge of the "enlightenment of the Soul" he is an ordinary being, like you and me.

Manushya's Sanskaras hmmmm, good & bad, some very good & some worst.

Manushya does not segregate the negative with the positive. Whatever comes his way, he accepts it. But, Manushya is learning, not only learning, getting the knowledge, but, also, adopting the knowledge and putting it into practice in daily life.

By error, or as Karmas have it, Manushya takes shelter in a Meditation hall to evade the nasty winds, gales, rain & thunderstorm.

Words come pouring in his ear. Manushya cocks his ears, someone is giving a discourse, he listens:

"...is totally different from the Gods we pray to in our normal course of life. To understand the reality of the Absolute is just banned to ordinary human beings. Those on a path towards Self, God-Realization get a glimpse of his domain now and then ... the divine link, which keeps the spark of self inquiry glowing within!

"How much blessed are those ... Who see the Almighty in all its Cosmic glory!! The most beautiful of the beautiful ... is but a creation of his ... be it the beauty of the Nature, Science or a Human being.

"One who can create such beauty ... a Cosmos comprising of many Universes, a Universe comprising of many Milky ways and Galaxies, Milky ways and Galaxies having cluster of Stars exceeding tens of thousand in numbers! Among the Stars a small Star with nine Planets is our Solar system!! What Cosmic beauty ... what display of accuracy and control!! Not a single Star or Planet going out of control and dashing against another upsetting the Cosmic order and balance ... You can now imagine how mighty would he be!!!

Is a puny human being supposed to question his propriety? The most frequently asked question (FAQ) ... Why were we created! to suffer at his hands!! What an anomaly!!! Why would he who created us would lead us astray only to suffer ... Such is not ... his being. We underestimate and under-evaluate him and continue doing our most heinous deeds! We try to shift the blame of our cowardice and inaction ... Still, the balance remains maintained.

Theory of Karma keeps the system of God perpetuating in full glory ... only to be rediscovered by an Avatar, a son of God after every 1000~2000 years! Only when such a mighty one unveils the Absolute Truth ... Do we shift the focus of blame from God to self and praise the Lord for what he is and shall continue to be.

"We talk about Brahmand (Cosmos), Brahmand stands for

the total Creation existing ... perceptible by our senses, science and beyond all comprehension up to the last stretches of entity covered by evolution.

To envision the vast area covered by total Cosmos, we have to start from the level of a human being. Human beings imagine and live within a notion that earth is the end of all. Comparing the planet Earth with the size of Cosmos we ultimately realize the absolute truth ... planet earth forms part of a cluster of nine planets revolving around sun, a small star. Millions of stars comprise a galaxy. Millions of Galaxies form one universe and thousands of universes constitute the entire structure the Brahmand (the Cosmos).

Relatively insignificant but the ability to achieve the status of man god ... such is the capability inherent in all human beings. One may or may not be able to achieve the ultimate goal in one life span of 70 - 80 years is but a matter of speculation and entirely dependent upon the resultant karma of a being.

Brahmand is considered to be without a boundary ... hence the saying by god realized souls that the ephemeral world is but a thought of God. All is Maya (ignorance). It is the ego within every being owing to which a Jivatma (soul + body) starts giving weight-age to the physical part of the self. Understand the Cosmic truth and all would become clear.

Relatively speaking, human being is but a speck of dust in the vast Cosmos yet most powerful. Why not scan the latent powers and realized self within this life!!"

Manushya is confused. He tries to talk to himself. Suddenly, a LIGHT! Me, I, Myself, where are these? In me, ofcourse. He mutters to himself. Where in me? Manushya is lost. He cannot sleep at night.

Dreams, has nightmares and is confused. How can he see himself when he is asleep. Where does he go when he is sleeping. If he goes somewhere unknown, that means, this physical body lies in the room where he is sleeping. This must be the death stage. But, then, Manushya thinks, this being, which goes and wanders, comes back. So, it must be a temporary death. Why can he not remember those dreams?

No. Manushya thinks of studying about "sleep and dreams" day & night. As luck would have it, Manushya receives some notes from "Dream Foundation" on Sleep, Dreams, (Lucid dreaming & Nightmares) and dream recall. Manushya starts reading:

Every person on earth dreams every night every mammal in fact. It follows then that something extremely important must be going on while we sleep and dream, yet in the industrialized world, the majority of people pay little attention to dreams, and sometimes shortchange themselves on sleep because it is perceived as lost time, or at best unproductive.

How astonishing that we generally ignore this third (and possibly far more) of ourselves. An appropriate analogy to the grandeur of this mass misunderstanding is the incredible inertia in the middle ages against the idea of earth being other than flat until repeated point-blank evidence like Galileo's observation of other planets and their moons and the journeys of Columbus' and other explorers across the ocean proved conclusively otherwise.

The challenge was that people's everyday experience contradicted the idea of a spherical earth because nobody had yet gained perspective from outside of the system. Airplanes and especially photographs from space were not yet available, so there was little first hand evidence of a new paradigm that was quite a great leap beyond the old.

Fortunately, people eventually began to come around, and the shift triggered an ensuing surge of exploration as the realization and acceptance finally dawned that our world really isn't flat after all.

Dreams, in the same way, encompass yet another entire dimension of experience, a world as yet unexplored by most, where a fascinating sphere of activity awaits investigation and possible harvest for greater fulfillment in waking life. The challenge is again the same common daily experience for the average person offers little proof of this other reality, let alone the possible value of this other dimension of experience, unless one can gain perspective from outside the 9-to-5 workday framework and a scientific purely-objective system.

Dream related mental skills such as dream recall or dream interpretation and information on subjects such as the meaning of nightmares or precognitive dreams isn't taught in our schools, and the majority of our parents knew or passed on little about the value of dreams as we grew up.

So it's no big surprise that many adults remember few or no dreams, and even more rarely contemplate or set out to interpret the guidance and mine the jewels of creative inspiration hidden just below the surface of consciousness in dreams. Basically, nobody told us or showed us how dreams can be extremely practical.

The result of where this long-standing trend of disregarding dreams has brought society is that the current misguided concepts about the value of dreams are not only crucial misunderstandings, but also represent and even bring about a lack of connection with the subconscious and our own deeper nature. This artificial rift may indirectly, or even rather directly be the source for many of our current personal, cultural and planetary social, political, and environmental challenges.

One solution towards rebalancing and integration on a personal and eventually a planetary level, is for each of us to realize and begin to investigate how our personal dreams, at very least, each night offer a direct means to explore inner reality and gain unique, undeniable experiences of deep personal value. Further, there is overwhelming evidence that they can be harvested to improve waking life, supporting Shakespeare's age-old claim by MacBeth that sleep and dreams are the "chief nourishers in life's feast". Dreams do indeed offer opportunities for fun, adventure, wish fulfillment, creativity, deep personal insight and healing and all this at no cost and with no line-ups!

Not only do dreams offer a private means to explore inner reality and to gain unique, undeniable, personal experiences, but there is overwhelming evidence that they can be used to improve waking life, often immeasurably, supporting Shakespeare's age-old claim by MacBeth that "they are chief nourishers in life's feast." Dreams offer opportunities for fun, adventure, wish fulfillment, creativity, deep personal insight and healing, and all this at no cost and with no line-ups!

As far back as recorded history and probably further, dreams have been employed for guidance and healing. The dream temples of ancient Greece are a classic example where the ill would perform a sacred ritual and sleep in a specialized healing temple. The Greek god Asklepios would often appear in a visionary dream, perform a symbolic operation, and the seeker would awaken healed or having received guidance.

Closer to home, many native American tribes such as the Ojibwa of the Great Lakes, have expanded their use of incubation beyond healing. Young adults would embark upon a dream or vision quest into the wilderness as a rite of passage into adulthood and would fast and pray until the anticipated dream was received. Blessed by the dream with guidance or revelations about latent personal talents, the youths would return to the tribe with the responsibility to apply and share their gifts for the benefit of the community.

The process of incubation is the basis for all the applications that follow. Although perhaps a forgotten art in our culture, it is innate and neither esoteric nor difficult, and often operates automatically as we fall asleep with a problem in mind. How often have you heard a friend with a pending decision, problem or question say, "Let me sleep on it"?

To consciously incubate a dream, simply hold your question or problem clearly in mind as you prepare for sleep. Then ask (rather than command) yourself to have and clearly remember a dream which reveals the answer as either an insight, an actual experience, or both. In the morning, record any dreams or thoughts which you have upon waking for later reflection. The answer may be obvious or may not be immediately apparent, but trust that the process is working and try to put any insights you get into practice.

This last step often involves drawing upon courage and self-discipline to face personal fears and/or overcome present personal limitations, but is important, as explained by the following analogy: if you ask someone for a gift and they grant your wish, they won't be overly impressed or nearly as generous next time if you lose, ignore or forget about it, so try to maintain a grateful appreciation for having received such guidance and it will likely promote further insight and future success.

"After learning about dream incubation, I suggested to myself to have a healing dream since I'd been feeling drained of energy for some time and had a bad cold coming on, which is unusual for me. I dreamt that the pores of my legs opened and ugly leeches oozed out. I awoke feeling much better. I never did find out exactly what it represented, but it sure worked." (M.S., Palo Alto, CA)

"I'm a tri-athlete. After an important, upsetting race where I biked and ran well below my capability, I decided to incubate a dream about it. After a week of focusing, I remembered this

dream: 'I'm with my coach discussing how I was so tight and cramped during the race. He suggests regular sports massages for the racing season and says he knows a guy who could do it.' When I awoke and phoned him, he confirmed the dream and connected me with his massage therapist. A few weeks later I won my first major race, becoming the New England Long Course Champion. Two weeks after that, I qualified for the World Championships in Hawaii." (R.C., Montreal, QC).

"A new relationship came into my life, except that communication suddenly broke off for a few days, so I asked for guidance from my dream as to whether this relationship would be healthy for me. That night, I dreamt I was trying to talk to my new boyfriend on the phone. The connection kept getting cut off his because his end of the line was made of many small bits of phone wire poorly patched together. The dream confirmed my feeling that keeping good communication with this new partner might prove difficult. On top of that, he even told me when he finally called a few days later that he wasn't yet ready to be close to anyone."

On Resolving Nightmares, Anxiety Dreams & Recurring Dreams.

Almost everyone has experienced one or more dreams that contain anxiety or outright fear. These experiences can be quite traumatic or become recurrent. For some, unpleasant dreams or nightmares repeat in actual content. For others, the content may change while the theme remains the same, such as scenes of falling, or of being pursued or attacked, of being late or unprepared for class, a presentation or an exam.

Some people even dream of being stuck in slow motion and unable to move, or of being naked in public, to name a few common themes. Research has shown that most recurring dreams are described as being unpleasant. Furthermore, many dream theories converge in their view that this type of experience is associated with lack of progress by the dreamer to recognize and solve related conflicts in life.

Fear of nightmares from early in life, or other anxieties or misguided beliefs about dreams and the unconscious can block dream recall. But, this can usually be overcome by learning about the useful nature of dreams and by recognizing that many nightmares, like a bitter but quite necessary medicine, represent opportunities for healing and insight. This can warn of psychological imbalances that we need to remedy, or of current behaviors or decisions which may soon become detrimental unless we change them.

"Some years ago I was a heavy cigarette smoker, up to two packs a day. Then one night I had an exceptionally vivid and realistic dream in which I had inoperable cancer of the lung. I remember as though it were yesterday looking at the ominous shadow in my chest X-ray and realizing that the entire right lung was infiltrated.

I experienced the incredible anguish of knowing my life was soon to end, that I would never see my children grow up, and that none of this would ever have happened if I had quit cigarettes when I first learned of their carcinogenic potential. I will never forget the surprise, joy, and exquisite relief of waking up. I felt I was reborn. Needless to say, the experience was sufficient to induce the immediate cessation of my cigarette habit."

Fortunately, there exist treatments for nightmares that do not involve medication and which have shown to be remarkably effective. Some of the most effective techniques presently being used in psychotherapy include voice dialogue work, dream lucidity, guided imagery, dream rehearsal.

Dream lucidity is a subject of current research with doctors at Montreal's Sacré Coeur Hospital Dream and Nightmare Laboratory. The lucid dreaming approach for resolving nightmares is demonstrated the following typical integration dream:

"After many recurring nightmares where I'm pursued by some terrifying figure, I learned of lucid dreaming and had the following dream: I'm in a frantic car chase with the pursuer right behind me. Swerving into a lot, I bolt out of the car and run with him hot on my heels.

Suddenly, the scene seems familiar and I realize that I'm dreaming, though the parking lot and trees still seem more real than ever. Drawing upon every ounce of courage that I have, I swirl to face my pursuer, repeating to myself that it's only a dream. Still afraid, I scream at him, "You can't hurt me!" He stops, looking surprised. For the first time I see his beautiful, loving eyes. "Hurt You?" he says. "I don't want to hurt you. I've been running after you all this time to tell you that I love you!" With that, he holds out his hands, and as I touch them, he dissolves into me. I awake filled with energy, feeling great for days. The nightmare never returned." (M.R., San Jose, CA).

A Rich Source of Creativity

Dreams have long proven themselves to be storehouses of creativity and may in fact be the well from which imagination springs. With dream incubation and the new opportunities presented by lucid dreaming, artists, musicians, dancers, sculptors, and inventors are able to dive deep into the source of inspiration and explore the vast reaches of their own creative potential by meeting face to face with the unconscious.

The increased clarity and directable nature of the lucid state often enables the dreamer to return awake weighed down with creative insights.

A Valuable Problem-Solving Tool

The tale is now famous of how, after an embarrassing slump, golfer Jack Nicklaus claims to have solved a problem with his golf swing within a dream, which subsequently improved his game by ten strokes -- overnight!

There are undoubtedly plenty more undocumented examples spread over history, but some well-documented ones include the dream-inspired experiment and resulting discovery of the chemical mediation of nerve impulses by Otto Leowi, which won him a Nobel prize, Elias Howe's discovery of the sewing machine, many of Thomas Edison's inventions and Friedrich Kekulé's discovery of the structure of the benzene ring from a hypnagogic dream where he saw a snake swallowing it's tail. Said an excited Kekulé to his colleagues, "Let us learn to dream!"

Physical & Professional Skill Rehearsal

German psychologist and **lucid dream** researcher Paul Tholey used dream work in his training of the German Olympic ski jumping team. He had the skiers learn lucid dreaming so that they could creatively experiment with new maneuvers, without risk of injury, and gain confidence in the most believable virtual environment available -- the world of dreams.

Dreams are also beginning to be used in this regard for improving business, and professional performance:

"After nursing school, I dreamed how I would manage a cardiac arrest and most anything stressful in my new career. I can make myself dream just about anything that I need to 'practice' before doing it." (C.A., Jacksonville, FL)

A medical student reported this lucid dream: *"Before I went to sleep, I was mulling over the ways in which I could present my internship experience to my classmates. While dreaming, and knowing I was dreaming, I wheeled a cart of stuff into the classroom, set it up, and did a wonderful presentation. I saw overheads outlining my talk, slides, posters - everything I would need. When I awoke, it was clear how I should organize and present the material, so I did, and it went beautifully." (M.K., Wildwood Crest, NJ)*

In dreams and in lucid dreams especially, where the world

avails itself to the desires of the dreamer, adventure and intrigue are almost guaranteed because the usual laws of physics and of society no longer apply, and many of the apparent blocks set by age, sex, race or religion simply fall away.

In dreams we can be the hero of our own adventure, find romance, fly, travel through "solid" objects, breathe underwater, and perform feats free from embarrassment, peer pressure, monetary limits, and even physical handicaps. The boundaries of imagination are the only limits. One can even follow in the footsteps of Tibetan monks who master lucid dreaming as a spiritual illumination stepping stone on the path to enlightenment.

"All my life I've taken wondrous adventures upon the wings of my imagination while dreaming. I have flown many nights, talked to bears, dogs, raccoons, and owls; I have swum with dolphins and whales, breathing underwater as if I had gills"

"I suddenly realize I'm dreaming from the surprise and excitement of recognizing that I've become a salmon swimming upstream! Leaping high into the air, I climb a series of chutes. Then I flip up onto the shore and the flipping sensation feels so odd that I soon awaken." (W.D., Palo Alto, CA)

"Falling asleep, I remember wondering what truly 'knowing myself' *would be like. Dreaming, I become aware of this incredible, indescribably powerful 'Love Light'. The thought comes that there is no power like it - it's absolutely non-judgmental, and dwarfs every worry or desire I've ever had. It is peace and simplicity and well-being. It includes sexuality but*

encompasses far more. Basking in what feels like 'an ocean of grace', I soon realize that I'm not looking at it, but rather that I AM it, recognizing myself."

Nightmares? Bad dreams, or, Recurring Dreams? *Lucky You!*

The above title may seem odd, if not a complete contradiction. Why would anyone suggest that nightmares or anxiety dreams might be helpful? If you're a part of more than half the population that has experienced an anxiety dream or nightmare within the last month, then this may even be what you're wishing you could get rid of, right? Some people who had nightmares or recurring dreams early on in life even manage to block their dream recall entirely in order to stop being upset by such experiences.

This unfortunate view of "bad" dreams as things to avoid is precisely the reason for the above title and for this article. An avoidance or denial approach is much like putting a Band-Aid on a car's blinking oil light because the light seems annoying. Of course fifty or a hundred miles later, it would be greatly preferable to have understood the warning.

Obviously, it's preferable not to have the light blinking, but if it does, then it's important to do something about it since it's there for a good reason -- one certainly wouldn't be very wise to disable it. Though perhaps not obvious, the simple fact is that most nightmares and almost all recurring dreams are similarly trying to provide an extremely valuable service to the dreamer. If we block them, we are likely missing their immediate benefit; if we remember but ignore them, we may well be missing the vital message that they are trying to bring us about our life.

Almost everyone has experienced one or more dreams that contain anxiety or outright fear. For some, unpleasant dreams or nightmares recur repeatedly; for others, the content may change while the theme remains the same, such as scenes of falling, or of being pursued or attacked, late or unprepared for a presentation or an exam, stuck in slow motion, unable to move or scream, or naked in public, to name a few common themes.

This type of experience, when unpleasant, is usually associated with lack of progress by the dreamer to recognize and solve related conflicts in life.

Though it has been scientifically proven that we all dream every night, fear of nightmares or other anxieties or misguided beliefs about dreams and the unconscious can block dream recall. This can usually be overcome by learning about the useful nature of dreams and by recognizing that the majority of nightmares, like a bitter but quite necessary medicine, represent opportunities for personal healing through much-needed emotional release. They are often indirectly warning us about current behavior patterns or psychological imbalances that we need to remedy if we don't want such unpleasant dreams to repeat, or worsen.

Sometimes, such imbalances or patterns resolve themselves as the dream percolates into waking thought and we unknowingly respond and make adjustments in our life. But if we block, deny or ignore such messages from the subconscious for too long, then it simply speaks 'louder' to get our attention often by bringing related events, which I call daymares, into our waking hours. These daymares show up as sickness, accidents, relationship difficulties or other unfortunate personal circumstances which now force us outright to deal with the issue at hand. Interestingly enough, such events often have repeating themes as well, such as recurring relationship patterns, for example.

Psychologist Ernest Rossi has put forth that one important function of dreaming is integration: the combining of separate psychological structures into a more balanced and comprehensive personality. Renown psychologist Carl Jung observed that portions of our whole personality which we knowingly or unknowingly judge become disowned, and are frequently projected outward in dreams, taking the form of aggressors, devils, monsters, intimidating animals or natural events (e.g. tidal waves), and so on.

Jung referred to these symbolic figures as "the shadow". Whether we become aware of such elements of our shadow through nightmares or daymares, re-accepting these judged and disowned portions of ourselves is the message and the awaiting gift.

So, we truly are lucky to have such nightmares, since they provide a natural 'pressure-release' therapy for the psyche, and especially since they may even provide what amounts to an early cure if we listen to, make an effort to understand and then act upon the valuable insight that dreams try to bring us. The goal is still to put an end to nightmares and recurring dreams, but by evolving them into more beneficial scenarios, and not by blocking, ignoring or denying them.

Resolving Nightmares

Fortunately, there exist treatments for nightmares that do not involve medication and which have shown to be remarkably effective. Some of the most useful techniques include dream rehearsal, dream lucidity, guided imagery and mainstream therapies such as gestalt, psychosynthesis, focusing, or other such methods.

I have no intention of providing an absolute dream dictionary (since dreamers and their experiences relating to specific symbols are so individual) and have no illusions about prescribing instantaneous solutions or cures, however a great number of people have gotten a lot of help and insight by learning about universal nightmare and anxiety dream themes which they are also experiencing. Here are some of the most common themes (with positive outcome examples for each scenario) and suggestions about what the dreamer might look at in waking life:

✍ The pursuer usually represents a fearful aspect of our shadow, and hence an exaggerated version of a denied or inhibited portion of our own personality that would benefit us if integrated and appropriately expressed. *(ideal outcome: standing our ground, facing and dialoguing with our pursuer, and eventually, acceptance and embrace)*

✍ falling dream : Am I feeling heavy, unsupported, worried about something? How can I feel freer, lighter? Also: do I need to be more grounded? *(ideal outcome: feeling safe, landing, floating or flying)*

✍ car out of control : Is life too hectic, out of control? How could I slow down, act more peacefully and "enjoy the ride"? *(ideal outcome: driving well & within speed limits, walking peacefully)*

✍ unprepared, late for or failing an exam : Am I feeling unprepared for some upcoming event? Unconfident about my performance? Am I worrying needlessly or do I actually need more preparation in order to feel confident and do a good job? *(ideal outcome: feeling assured about oneself, performing well)*

✍ stuck in slow motion, unable to move or make any noise: Where am I feeling stuck in life, like I'm getting nowhere or unable to voice my true feelings? What can I do to change it? *(ideal outcome: relaxation and acceptance, and eventually, peaceful action & self-expression)*

✍ embarrassed to be nude or naked in public, though nobody seems to notice or mind: Where in life am I feeling unconfident, embarrassed, unskilled? This type of dream is usually pointing out, by the fact that the other characters in the dream don't seem to notice, that we are the only one viewing our self this way, and usually mistakenly so. *(ideal outcome: comfortable with oneself as is, confident)*

✍ personal injury, dismemberment : What part of my lifenot usually the physical bodyhave I been neglecting, mistreating, forgettingi.e. dis-membering as opposed to remembering? *(ideal outcome: healing)*

✍ trapped, locked in: Where am I feeling trapped in life? How might I open myself up to a new perspective, and explore new courses of action? *(ideal outcome: breaking out, exploration)*

✍ drowning, threatening waves, tsunami (tidal waves) or flooding: Am I blocking, denying or feeling overwhelmed by my emotions? How might I better acknowledge, accept, and feel these feelingswhich often include vulnerability? *(ideal outcome: swimming, surfing, breathing underwater)*

✍ helpless, abandoned, or crying baby, monkey, bunny or small animal: Have I been taking care of my "inner child"? Maybe I need to laugh more, play outdoors, express my creativity, be more spontaneous, or enjoy more personal warmth and intimacy? *(ideal outcome: caring for baby or animal, playing, simply having fun)*

Precognitive Dreams, Premonitions & Warning Dreams

Though they are generally symbolic of psychological processes, some dreams and nightmares are intended as guidance or warnings on a very practical level. For example, if you were to dream about the brakes failing on your car, it might help to ponder whether you are figuratively having trouble "slowing yourself down" in your life, however, it would also be very wise to check the actual brakes on your automobile in waking life.

Assuredly, not all precognitive dreams are about dire events, though when they are, such nightmares or anxiety dreams warn of current behavior trends, courses of action, or decisions which may soon become detrimental unless we change them, as exemplified in this dream by Stanford University pioneer sleep researcher Dr. William Dement:

"Some years ago I was a heavy cigarette smoker, up to two packs a day. Then one night I had an exceptionally vivid and realistic dream in which I had inoperable cancer of the lung. I remember as though it were yesterday looking at the ominous shadow in my chest X-ray and realizing that the entire right lung was infiltrated. I experienced the incredible anguish of knowing my life was soon to end, that I would never see my children grow up, and that none of this would ever have happened if I had quit cigarettes when I first learned of their carcinogenic potential.

I will never forget the surprise, joy, and exquisite relief of waking up. I felt I was reborn. Needless to say, the experience was sufficient to induce the immediate cessation of my cigarette habit."

Somehow, dreams have access to information above and beyond the physical senses, both in terms of geography and time. Exactly how this is possible is an extremely interesting question, both for the individual who has such experiences, and, in general, for the scientific communitywhere a solely objective investigative approach often misses a lot of valuable clues about the nature of reality, especially when it comes to the realm of subjective experiences such as dreams.

My view is that the state of consciousness from where our dream experiences arise is not the same as the "normal" physical waking state (which varies a great deal also), and so perceptions which come to us from such a state (and similarly with meditation, and even day-dreaming and deep states of creativity) arise from a framework beyond our physical one, and hence come from outside our normal framework of time and space.

Therefore, it is actually no great surprise and even somewhat common (especially with dreams) that we can sense, through a faculty other than the five physical senses, information which, within the physical world is either ahead or long past in terms of time, unavailable to us in terms of physical location or geography, or unknown to us though others in our life are aware of such information.

Catholic Bishop Joseph Lanyl dreamed of the assassination of the arch-duke of Austria, François-Ferdinand de Habsbourg. In vain, he tried to reach the arch-duke to warn him of the assassination, which occurred June 28, 1914 in Sarajevo the event that triggered the first world war.

A few days before his assassination, American President Abraham Lincoln, who was very attentive to his dreams, dreamt of his own corpse laid out in a room in the white house.

A day before the Titanic's demise, a woman on the infamous ship dreamt of the horrible event that was to occur the next day. She told her husband, who scoffed at her worries and ignored her pleas. However, the dream so affected her that she secretly prepared herself the night before and had all her children sleep in their warm clothes in order to be ready at a moment's notice. During the night, when the ship struck the iceberg, she and her children managed to escape and be rescued. Her husband, sadly, went down with the ship.

That it is possible to know about future events not only courts the disbelief of skeptics, but also often scares people who have such precognitive dreams. Such experiences are actually somewhat common, so people's apprehension is rather unfortunate, because the cultivation of such dreams can really be a beneficial skill, much like a natural talent in music or writing or dance, and can truly become a helpful gift developed both for the benefit of the dreamer and for those around him or her, as shown by this dreamer's premonition:

"I had a dream where my father had blood pouring out of an eye from an accident involving the machine he was working with, and I knew he had lost his eye. Upon awakening, I immediately phoned my parents and asked my father what he was planning that day. He said he was going to work in his workshop with his drill and circular saw. Hearing this, I strongly urged him and eventually got him to promise to wear safety goggles while he was working.

Then I spoke to my mother, told her the dream, and convinced her to keep a close eye on Dad. That night, Dad phoned in disbelief to tell me that a piece of wood had flown off the saw right at his eye and shattered the safety glasses. He was very grateful and admitted to me that it was truly a miracle that his eye was untouched." (S.B. Montreal, Qc)

So instead of wishing you sweet dreams, which you've heard many times before, I will go one step further, with your greatest fulfillment in mind, and wish you truly pleasant nightmares.

RECURRING DREAM & NIGHTMARE RESOLUTION EXERCISE : RE-SCRIPTING A DREAM (Ex. 1)

Select a nightmare or upsetting dream which you've recently had (especially if it happened this morning!) and either from the recurring dream suggestions above or on your own, re-design a different ending to the dream. Choose something which leaves you feeling empowered, free and confident, and great about the new scenario, instead of the way you felt during or after the actual dream.

Before lying down to fall asleep tonight, sit in a comfortable position and relax your body and mind completely for a couple minutes. It may help you to alternately tense and relax different parts of your body, and witness instead of concentrate upon any thoughts which cross your mind. Let it all go until tomorrow. Then, once you're calm and quiet, mentally visualize or remember the dream you've selected for this exercise, running through as though you were watching a video, except at the point where things begin to turn unpleasant, replace the old ending with the new empowering one you created earlier, and imagine it as vividly as you can, "making it up" as you go if you need to.

Make it a special point to experience the new feelings of confidence, freedom and empowerment that your new ending gives you. Then give yourself the clear suggestion that not only are these new thought patterns now spreading into your waking life, but also that tonight or some time soon you may have just such a dream, which includes the new, more fulfilling ending.

You may even suggest to yourself that you will recognize the dream as a dream, while it's happening, in which case you can consciously direct it as you feel appropriate towards a more uplifting outcome.

RECURRING DREAM & NIGHTMARE RESOLUTION EXERCISE : RE-SCRIPTING A DREAM (Ex. 2)

Dreams are an easy and natural way to pursue spiritual unfoldment. Here is an exercise you can try before you go to sleep. It can help you see your problems from a higher viewpoint to aid you in your life.

Make a request. Before you go to sleep, write down a question about a problem that bothers you. Ask the Dream Master or your own spiritual teacher for guidance on this question. Lie down, and close your eyes.

Sing HU. Softly sing HU (pronounced like the word *hue*) for about five minutes. HU is an ancient name for God. It has the unique ability to lift you into a higher state of awareness. Singing HU connects you with Divine Spirit, or ECK, which can be seen as an inner light or heard as sound.

Write down your experiences. When you wake up in the morning, write down any dreams, thoughts, or feelings, even if you don't think they are significant. As you go through your day, write down any new thoughts or experiences that relate to your problem. Do this for three to five days. Then look over your notes. You may discover that images you first thought were unrelated now make sense and give you clues to the overall pattern of your life.

Lucid Dreaming & Dream Consciousness

Although science has proven that we all dream every night, many people often remember no dreams at all, and even when they do, it is almost exclusively upon awakening, *after the fact*.

Lucid dreams are uniquely different. One realizes that one is dreaming *while the dream is still happening*. The scene often suddenly expands in richness and color as the dreamer becomes aware that the world being experienced, although appearing utterly real and believable, is only a dream and that she or he is actually safe asleep in bed. With this new understanding, the lucid dreamer is free to explore remarkable worlds limited only by imagination, and now not just as an actor, but also to some degree as a producer and director.

Lucid dreaming was brought into the academic and public spotlights around the world once it's scientific validity was separately proven by researchers at Stanford University, California (where *it has also been proven to be a learnable skill*), and at Liverpool University, England. Proof was achieved by performing, during REM sleep, a series of extreme left-right eye signals which were agreed upon prior to sleep. Though most of the body's muscles are de-activated during REM sleep, the eye muscles are not, and repeated experiments at Stanford, the Sacré-Coeur Hospital Dream and Nightmare Laboratory and elsewhere have proven that the eyes (and to some extent other physiological responses) can be brought under conscious control by a dreamer who realizes that she or he is dreaming.

Lucid Dreaming Techniques

Here's a brief look at some of the best techniques for bringing the light of lucid awareness to your dreams. This isn't meant to replace a committed, consistent effort, or reading books on the subject such as *Creative Dreaming* , or *Exploring the World of Lucid Dreaming*, but perhaps it can serve as a jumping off point for those who want to efficiently focus their efforts without delay.

Some techniques are less suitable to a regular daily work schedule, however, the more you can focus on the various techniques and lucid dreaming in general, the more frequent will be your lucid dreams.

Master dream recall: No other practice is more effective. The main barrier to realizing when one is dreaming is that our waking and dreaming minds are not connected nearly as much as they could be with simple intention, practice and focus.

Making a consistent effort to remember dreams will help your waking mind to ally itself more closely with your dreaming awareness and will also allow you to become more familiar with your personal dream content - characters, settings, feelings or sensations that seem odd (though only after you awaken) because they're often not a usual part of your waking experience. This will then allow your waking reasoning and reflective capabilities to be more present in dreams so that you recognize unfamiliar or unlikely surroundings or feelings while you're still actually experiencing them in a dream.

Success with lucid dreaming is most likely if you recall one dream or more per night, in fact you may already be having lucid dreams and simply not remembering them. So, to increase dream recall: As you go to bed, clearly ask yourself to remember your dreams when you awaken in the morning or during the night. When you do awaken, keep your eyes closed (or shut them if already opened) and remain as motionless as possible.

Gather as any images, feelings or impressions as you can and then rise and quickly jot them down in a notebook (which you keep bedside), no matter how brief or vague they may at first seem. You'll be surprised at how much more you begin to remember as you write. This is also an excellent way to increase intuitive capabilities, since dreaming and intuition are closely related.

Arise during the night: Research has proven that morning naps after a period of wakefulness are extremely productive times for lucid dreaming. This is for (at least) 3 reasons:

(a) We have more REM (dream) activity per sleep cycle as the night progresses (i.e. more dreams, more chance of a lucid dream),

(b) There's much less time between when we fall asleep and when REM sleep begins than at the start of the night (about 90 minutes compared to 5-20 minutes during a morning nap), so we have more chance of bridging the wake-sleep "forget-as-you-pass-by" barrier,

(c) We tend to sleep more lightly (with much less or no deep sleep) as the morning approaches.

This technique probably requires the most motivation, but also provides the best pay-off. Week-ends or vacation are a particularly good time to try it. The best method is to arise either 1½ or 3 hours (1 or 2 sleep cycles) earlier than usual, stay awake for 30-90 minutes, and then return to bed for the remainder of your postponed sleep. During the period of wakefulness, it's important to "get awake" to some degree. Some of the best activities for this period are: taking a midnight walk (lots of fun!), lovemaking, and especially meditation (Vipassana technique is particularly good). Ideally, anything that brings or maintains presence of mind.

Visualization (MILD) technique: This technique is extremely effective, although it can be difficult to focus upon since it's practiced while falling asleep. The basics are: Before going to bed, use the autosuggestion method for promoting good dream recall and the occurrence of lucid dreams, and then (ideally) use the following technique on a previous night's dream: When you awaken after any REM period, arouse yourself and recall as many dreams as possible using the dream recall methods.

Before returning to sleep (while sitting on the side of your bed is best so as not to doze off before finishing the technique), tell yourself "*The next time I'm dreaming, I want to remember that I'm dreaming*", then imagine you are back in the dream from which you just awoke, remembering it step by step, scene by sœne, except that this time you see yourself recognizing that you're dreaming (ideally when something odd occurs) and carrying out some planned activity (see below). Then lay down, and focus upon your intention followed by the visualization as many times as you can until you fall asleep.

re-scripting a dream (ex. 2)

Stay present as you drift asleep: As you lie ready for sleep, especially after waking during the night, focus upon your breath and simply observe any thoughts that arise, without getting caught by them. If you do, and later "snap back", focus right back on your breath.

Autosuggestion: As you go to bed, or if you awaken during the night, put yourself in the frame of mind of genuinely expecting that tonight or sometime soon you will become conscious within a dream. Clearly convince yourself in a friendly, assured (rather than pressured) way, and then let it go like a balloon. The Lucidity Institute's "Trance Induction of Lucid Dreaming" cassette can be helpful with this.

Plan a lucid dream activity: Realizing that you are dreaming is exciting - the thrill is great, but can also awaken you, especially if you're not sure what to do next. Imagine you've really been focusing for three weeks and all of sudden you realize you're dreaming, only to awaken from excitement. It's quite common - unless you have some specific activity to focus on right away. To continue past those first few moments of lucidity, plan in advance something specific to do in your next lucid dream. Many people choose flying, but the options are truly limitless. Let your imagination take you. The best activities for maintaining a lucid dream are those that engage you in the dream scenario.

Perform reality checks as a habit: Always *Test First and then Decide* when you have even the slightest inclination that you might be dreaming. In this way you won't miss valuable lucid opportunities. Also, throughout the day, ask yourself as often as you can remember, whether you are dreaming, and perform a test to find out. This may seem silly, but it will carry over by habit to the dream state, and you will be very glad (for once) when you find that your check has bounced!

The best test is to read some text, look away and quickly look back. If the words change - you are dreaming! It helps to try to get the words to change. A digital watch is excellent for this. If there is no text nearby, look at your hands for a good 5-10 seconds to see if they appear wavy or odd in any way - as they most often do in dreams.

Be patient and persistent: Although many people experience success the first night or during the first couple of weeks, lucid dreaming is a skill that requires time and focus to master. In this regard it's more like learning a sport or musical instrument rather than learning to ride a bike where you get it from one day to the next for good. Try to maintain a relaxed and playful attitude of looking forward to your dreams while being willing to let it happen all in good time.

Trying too hard or being too serious can be limiting factors. Dream recall, lucid dreams and even motivation all tend to come and go naturally in cycles, and also depend upon what else is going on in our lives. Continued practice of these techniques over at least a few months is more likely to bring mastery than a few intense but sparse attempts - *a weekly study group of people with a like interest is unmatchable for sustained motivation and inspiration.*

Once you start on a cycle of focusing on some of the

exercises, stick with it for *at least* a four or five days, because consecutive nights seem to have an additive effect.

Keep your life in balance: The subtle energies, ideology and realizations connected with lucid dreams and related experiences are very powerful and often of profound waking influence, at least psychologically. The approach of "as-much-lucidity-as-possible-as-fast-as-possible" is strongly discouraged. Such an approach can bring great imbalances and even unnecessary calamities into your waking life. There's no need for fear, but do remain aware of this important point.

Remember that trees stand as tall and withstand storms only as deep as their roots go, so stay grounded and maintain a healthy outward daily focus. To help regain balance if trouble arises, eat and sleep well, and maintain social connections. Other suggestions include getting a massage, going for extended exercise outdoors, and focusing on simple day-to-day tasks and therefore removing your focus from dreams and inner life for a while.

Dream Research, Sleep Disorders & Science of Dreams

In 1953, Eugene Aserinsky of the University of Chicago noticed that the eyes of sleeping babies moved beneath their eyelids at certain regular intervals. This led to the discovery of REM (Rapid Eye Movement) sleep periods, which occur at roughly 60-90 minute intervals throughout the night and which contain the dreams which are the most vivid and most often remembered. Since then, EEG (electroencephalogram) recordings, which monitor brain activity during sleep, have been used to map the various stages of sleep. These states are classified roughly into sleep onset (hypnagogia or stage 1), non-REM sleep (deep sleep or stages 2,3, and 4), and REM (or paradoxical) sleep.

Sleep-Related Disorders

Other than nightmares, there are various sleep disorders, which affect significant portions of the population.

Insomnia, the inability to fall asleep or get enough sleep, affects up to 20% of people. It is often triggered by stress and results in worrying that inhibits proper sleep.

Sleep apnea, actual lapses of breathing during sleep (mainly during REM sleep), is another common disorder often connected with obesity and/or intense snoring which results in excessive sleepiness during the day. It is harder to diagnose outside of the lab because the patient's asleep while it happens and has little way of knowing about the source of the trouble (though devices have now been developed for home diagnosis).

Sleep Paralysis is relatively common though rarely as a severe disorder. It occurs during sleep when a person partially awakens but is completely unable to move for some period after waking. It can be somewhat frightening, though there is no particular danger involved.

Parasomnias are a class of disorders which include nightmares (which often occur during long REM periods), sleep walking and sleep talking, bed-wetting, body rocking during sleep onset and teeth grinding (which all occur during non-REM sleep, the latter often being identifiable by worn down teeth or a sore jaw). Night terrors are also in this class, and differ from nightmares in that they occur during non-REM sleep and are usually very intense so that the sleeper awakes in panic, often screaming, with heart pounding, and with less recall of dream content.

Narcolepsy, often connected with sleep paralysis and vivid, frightening dreams at sleep onset, is characterized by irresistible daytime sleep attacks and collapsing at the onset of strong emotions (known as cataplexy) while remaining conscious (and so should not be confused with fainting).

Manushya is now equipped with the techniques to conrol and recall dreams. What should he do? The first thing he tries to do is to see himself being born. Day one of his birth.

Days turn into nights and nights to weeks, weeks to months. With one-track mind, Manushya tries and feeds the affirmation every night before sleeping. Then, it happens, he sees everything, the doctors, the nurses, the operation room, the equipment. Manushya sees himself as a baby, coming head first from the womb, from darkness to light.

Manushya is happy. He is gaining knowledge fast. Manushya is now 18 years of age.

Manushya knows, that Sages and Saints lived for hundreds of years, whilst the ordinary folk lived for only hundred plus years. What was it that kept them alive for so long. The quest continues. Manushya wants to learn everything, but, he also knows, time is short. Manushya approaches a Sufi on the outskirts of his village.

On approaching the Sufi saint, Manushya prostrates and asks "Oh, holy one, what is Celibacy? What is Kundalini? How do I increase my age and live a longer and fruitful life? Please give me, with your wisdom, Oh, Holy one."

The Sufi saint looks at Manushya. Smiles and tells him to sit and listen attentively.

Manushya listens attentively at the discourse:

THE DISCOURSE: -

Brahmacharya vrat (Vow of Celibacy)

"To answer your questions, son, I request you to be of one mind, one body and one spirit. Let not your mind waver. Listen to the words of wisdom and as you listen, experience the lesson you are being given today, with the grace of the Almighty.

We start from Brhamacharya vrat, which is the most fundamental requirement to be followed truthfully, sincerely and honestly for a period of full twelve years in continuation. A single break would render the austere practice useless. All would have to be repeated again. Sage Vishwamitra fell from grace and had to undergo the rigorous practice again when he got attracted towards a lady taking bath in the most sensuous environment ... by the lake in a forlorn jungle. Had he practiced control at this stage, he would have equaled Sage Vashisht but so was not to be.

In the present World full of lust and passions, to practice and be able to achieve the requisite vow would be short of a miracle. Yogis are not born. They make themselves so by performing penances of the highest order.

For the Kundalini to be awakened fully, practice of celibacy is a must. Awakening of Kundalini brings with itself many powers, foremost of which is ... darshan (vision) of God, the Creator. Coming face-to-face with your Atman (the soul within) gives you such an exhilarating experience that you can now weigh all your thinking and decisions on the Cosmic scale. Next, you achieve the power to invoke Cosmic wisdom (Jnana) available in the Brahmand (Cosmos) through the process of Sruti.

The present life becomes your last manifestation and there is no more life after death. You have been able to crossover from the threshold of death into the laps of God. What more could you ask for! The bodily manifestation having lost its value you start perceiving all as living Atmans (souls). Corresponding with live Atmans becomes a fancy for you. You take the charge of a preceptor and guide the humanity to its destined course.

What a glory awaits one who has taken complete control of self and having practiced celibacy for full twelve years becomes a direct son of God on mother Earth. Wow to such a one in whose glory basks complete humanity.

This is what the great Creator Brahma spoke to his children who are called the Prajapatis,Marichi, Asvini, Kasyapa, Angirasa, and others. This Knowledge has come down through *Guru-parampara* and not through books. Books cannot give this knowledge. By word of mouth has this knowledge been communicated. "Brahma spoke to Prajapatis." Here too, there is difference of opinion in regard to the interpretation of the meaning of the Upanishadic words. What is meant by saying that Brahma spoke to Prajapati?

It may be that the supreme Brahman spoke to the creator Hiranyagarbha also known as Brahma. Or it may be that Narayana spoke to Brahma as we hear it in the Srimadbhagavata, for instance. Or, according to Sankaracharya who has commented on the Upanishad, Brahma, the Creator, spoke to Kasyapa and other progenitors of the family of the universe who are known as Prajapatis. And these Prajapatis spoke to Manu, the first man, the Adam of our Creation. Then Manu gave this knowledge to others. So it has gradually come, stage by stage, from Guru to disciple, and finally to us.

Now, in this concluding passage of the Upanishad, we are given the advice that for the sake of this Knowledge one has to dedicate the whole of one's life in a highly disciplined manner. This vocation, if you would like to call it, is not going to be one among the many other activities in life.

It is a whole-souled aspiration, and so it calls for an application of every faculty of ours in a completely dedicated manner. What we usually call the four stages of life, the *asramas,brahmacharya,* (celibate student's life), *garhasthya* (married householder's life), *vanaprastha* (life of an anchorite), and *sannyasa* (monkhood)are hinted at in this passage as the requisite process through which one passes for the maturity of one's mind. And at the same time, a caution also is administered that the whole of one's life has to be lived in such a way that it is a preparation for the spiritual goal.

There is often a misconception that the spiritual part of one's life is *sannyasa* alone and the earlier three stages are not. This is what is refuted by all the Upanishads. All the stages of life right from *brahmacharya* onwards are preparations for spiritual life. Rather, all of them are necessary stages in one's ascent to the spiritual goal. It is not that the spiritual life commences only from *sannyasa* abruptly, as it were, and the earlier three stages are disconnected entirely from the spiritual goal. The whole of one's life from birth to death is a spiritual preparation. There is nothing but the Atman, the Spirit in life, and, therefore, no activity can be entirely secular, in the sense of its being bereft of the awareness of God's presence, as one's goal of life.

In India particularly we have what are called *samskaras*, the various ceremonies symbolic of the affiliation of every stage of one's life to the spiritual goal. There is no such thing as an unspiritual aspect of life, whether it be *brahmacharya, grahasthya,* or *vanaprastha.* This is a very important advice by which we are told that the whole life of a person, whoever be that person, is an entirely dedicated schooling, as it were, a period of training for the purpose of the final achievement of Liberation. There is no part of life which can be squandered or wasted, or completely cut off from this consciousness of the ideal of one's life.

Even childhood has to be associated by proper means. The moment consciousness becomes self-conscious even in a youngster; the traditional method is to be followed. He gets admitted into the *gurukula* of the *acharya*, the Guru. The sacred training ground is called the *gurukula*, the abode of the Guru, the atmosphere of a spiritual teacher. There one studies the Vedas. The Vedas are not studied as we are accustomed to study them these days. It is not merely a parrot-like chant of the words of the Vedas without knowing what they mean. Study of the Vedas is imbibing of knowledge, not merely a committing to memory of the words contained therein. And the Veda does not mean merely a book or a particular scripture. *Ananta Vedah* "Vedas are endless" says an old adage.

The Veda is a name given to the repository of all comprehensive knowledge which in turn has various stages and aspects of approach. Very few people have time enough to comprehend everything that is in the Veda. Most often they are introduced into certain *sakhas,* sections only, and even all those sections cannot be studied. Even if all those sections are taught, everything that is contained in them cannot be absorbed into one's mind. However, this study of the Veda is a very necessary stage of training.

There is another important advice here which is likely to miss the attention of ordinary people. The study under a preceptor should be done during the period of time which one has, apart from the time one spends for the service of the Guru. The student will not be studying from morning till evening sitting with a book, completely ignoring his duty of serving the Guru. Study is secondary and is to be undergone only at other times, the time of recess, as it were, which is at his disposal after he has completed his daily duties to his Guru.

Having undergone this training for the required period under a Guru, one usually enters the household life. The life of a householder should not be one of distracted secular activity. It is not the opposite of *sannyasa,* as people generally think. It is like *brahmacharya*, one of the steps leading to *sannyasa,* and at the same time, is the most mature part of one's life. There is a manifoldness of duty enjoined upon the householder.

His difficulties are many and, therefore, the training that he undergoes in that period is more effective, and is a greater preparation, as it were, than in any other stages. Having settled in a proper household after his period of training under a Guru is over, one should find time to be seated in a holy or sacred place and continue the study in order not to forget study, because it is the art of keeping the mind impressed with the consciousness of the goal of life. Else one will forget everything.

Though one may have studied something in the earlier days, one may forget everything and the mind may get rusted. *Svadhyaya* is a necessary perpetual training for everyone, which is not actually the process of acquiring new knowledge, but a way of keeping the mind aware always of what it has studied, and the way of applying this knowledge in practice to attain the great goal. So *svadhyaya* is a permanent requisite.

Always you have to be studying these great texts lest you may forget your goal. A householder has of, course, virtuous children or virtuous disciples who will receive this knowledge from him. Under him they undergo this kind of training. Thus he fulfils his obligation as a householder for the required period.

Then comes the stage of *vanaprastha.* Here he withdraws his senses. All the activities get centered in the Self when the senses are withdrawn. Instead of external activity, there is now internal activity. A psychological function replaces all the physical duties such as sacrifices, the *panchamahayajnas.* The various services that he was rendering outwardly in the world previously now become the responsibilities of his life in an internal world of self-control and withdrawal of the senses.

The great vow of the *sannyasin* is *ahimsa,* that he would never harm anyone. He is the embodiment of the great fearlessness that he extends to all living beings. No one will be afraid of seeing a *sannyasin,* for he will not do any harm or anything bad, as his heart has expanded beyond the limits of his own body and his family.

The term *anyatra tirthebhyah* here used with reference to *ahimsa* means that it would be difficult to extend this obligation of non-injury in an unconditional manner on account of the fact that we live in a world. Various interpretations have been offered for this particular phrase. The usual meaning would be the sacrificial injunctions of the Brahmanas of the Vedas that the committing of *himsa* is forbidden everywhere except in prescribed places or prescribed occasions.

The more generous interpretation of it, as is offered by many commentators, is that the prescribed occasions are those times or periods of activity when you are likely to commit some kind of harm to creatures inadvertently, as it were. It is not possible to live a life of such an extreme type of *ahimsa* on account of our not being aware many a time as to what we are doing. Of course the intention is not that you should consciously do any harm. Unconsciously harm is done.

This is done particularly by the householders because of their living in a house having a kitchen with a fire place, a water place, a grinding place, a broom, etc., where insects, flies and the like are likely to be crushed and killed inadvertently. Various other occasions also are there in life which cannot be recounted here when you are likely to cause unconsciously harm to living beings. These of course are excluded, if they are unconsciously done. But they can be expiated by the intense *sadhana* which the *sannyasin* is expected to perform in the purely internal spiritual life that he lives full of proper meditation.

The whole of one's life should be lived like this. The moment one becomes conscious of the goal of one's life, then it is up to one to see that one's every activity is somehow or other reconciled with this goal. One should not do any incompatible thing against one's own conscience and against the purpose that one has on hand. Thus it is that it is necessary to have one's entire life transformed into a spiritual art and complete dedication.

Often it is said that the last thought is the determining factor of one's future fate. The last thought that may come to the mind at the time of death is the fruit of this tree of the long life that one has lived in this world. We know very well that the fruit cannot be different from the nature of the tree.

So, the last thought cannot be something quite contrary to or different from the various impressions produced in the mind by the continuous thoughts that it was entertaining throughout life. And if one has to have this spiritual ideal maintained in one's consciousness at the time of departing, then it has to be maintained as a discipline throughout one's life.

Thus one reaches the great abode of the Creator, *Brahma-loka,* from whence there is no return. Once we go there, we will not come back. This is very frightening to many people. They interject: "We don't come back! Is it like entering into a lion's den!" We need not enter into this subject, because it looks very funny that after studying the whole Upanishad we have an uncanny fear that God will swallow us and we will have no occasion to come back. The question of coming back does not arise because we become one with the universal Reality. This going and coming are only ways of speaking in this phenomenal world. What happens is actually a union of consciousness with the All-Being, the Absolute.

These are the teachings of "The Chhandogya Upanishad" concludes the Sufi Saint. "Son, I have given you the nectar of life. How one should live life and how life should be, do you have any doubts?"

"No, Oh Holy one. Let me ponder and take-in what the gems, pearls and the navratnas you have poured to me. Let me think, how I am to use the wisdom imparted by you, oh Holy one"

The Sufi-Saint smiled.

Twelve years have passed. Manushya is now 30 years of age.

Manushya has completed the Gurukul stage of complete celibacy. His marriage has been confirmed. Manushya looks into the mirror of yesteryears. He had done many mistakes, made many bad Karmas. Manushya reflects, one bad karma leads to another one. He had tried to stop this chain of bad karma, with the nectar given by the Sufi Saint, Manushya treaded into life slowly.

Manushya had gone through the N.D.E. experiences on his own. N.D.E. standing for 'Near Death Experience". And, life is teaching Manushya quickly. What he thinks, materializes. In this cases, there is a seminar on 'N.D.E.' Manushya attends the seminar.

At the seminar.

The lecture had started. The speaker loud and clear voice, traveled easily across the hall.

Manushya listened.

Near Death Experience is what the words relate to. An experience where you have been declared dead by your doctor, and, you have seen or experienced or felt or imagined or visualized something which is beyond conception of any ordinary mind"

One study found that 8 to 12 percent of 344 patients resuscitated after suffering cardiac arrest had NDEs and about 18% remembered some part of what happened when they were clinically dead.

A wide array of experiences reported by some people who

have nearly died or who have thought they were going to die. There is no single shared experience reported by those who have had NDEs. Even the experiences of most interest to parapsychologists--such as the "*mystical experience*," the "*light at the end of the tunnel*" experience, the "*life review*" experience, and "*the out-of-body experience*"--rarely occur together in near-death experiences. However, the term NDE is most often used to refer to an OBE (Out of Body) occurring while near death.

Two M.D.s who have popularized the idea that the NDE is proof of life after death are Elizabeth Kübler-Ross and Raymond Moody. The former is well known for her work on death and dying. The latter has written several books on the subject of life after life, and has comprised a list of features he considers to be typical of the near-death experience. According to Moody, the typical NDE includes a buzzing or ringing noise, a sense of blissful peace, a feeling of floating out of one's body and observing it from above, moving through a tunnel into a bright light, meeting dead people, saints, Christ, angels, etc.; seeing one's life pass before one's eyes; and finding it all so wonderful that one doesn't want to return to one's body.

This composite experience is based on interpretations of testimonials and anecdotes from doctors, nurses, and patients. Characteristic of Moody's work is the glaring omission of cases that don't fit his hypothesis. If Moody is to be believed, no one near death has had a horrifying experience.

There are numerous reports of bad NDE trips involving tortures by elves, giants, demons, etc. Some parapsychologists take these good and bad NDE trips as evidence of heaven and hell. They believe that some souls actually leave their bodies and go to the other world for a time before returning to their bodies. If so, then what is one to conclude from the fact that most people near death do not experience either the heavenly or the diabolical? Is that fact good evidence that there is no afterlife or that most people end up in some sort of limbo? Such reasoning is on par with supposing that dreams in which one appears to oneself to be outside of one's bed are to be taken as evidence of the soul or mind actually leaving the body during sleep.

What little research there has been in this field indicates that the experiences Moody lists as typical of the NDE may be due to brain states triggered by cardiac arrest and anesthesia (Blackmore 1993). Furthermore, many people who have not been near death have had experiences that seem identical to NDEs. These mimicking experiences are often the result of psychosis (due to severe neurochemcial imbalance) or drug usage, such as hashish, LSD or DMT.

While neural activity might explain bright lights, buzzing noises, and hallucinations, there are some aspects of some NDEs that still remain puzzling. Some people who are thought to be dead, but are actually just unconscious, recover and remember things like looking down and seeing their own bodies being worked on by doctors and nurses. They recall conversations being held while they were "dead." Of course, they weren't dead at all, but they feel as if their mind or soul had left their body and was observing it from above.

Those who have had such experiences--and they are many--

often find them life-altering and defining moments. They are convinced such experiences are proof of life after death by a disembodied consciousness. But are they? It is possible that a person may appear dead to our senses or our scientific equipment but still be perceiving. The visual and auditory perceptions occurring while unconscious-but-perceiving may be produced by a variety of neuronal mechanisms. It is possible that the soul leaves the body, but it is not necessary to posit a soul to explain these experiences.

Raymond Quigg Lawrence (*Blinded by the Light*) thinks that NDEs are the work of Satan. Perhaps. Or, they may be telepathic communications from doctors, nurses, or others in attendance when the subject is near death. Or, they may be mixed memories composed after waking up and hearing others talk about what was happening while one was near death. Or, they may be recollections of subconsciously recorded data overheard while in a groggy state. At this point in our knowledge, to claim that NDEs provide proof that the soul exists independently of the body seems very premature.

I would like to give a few case studies:

"Jan. 8 — When a car plowed into the vehicle in which she was riding, Angela's chest was crushed, fourteen bones were broken and her heart stopped beating for fourteen minutes. Before she was revived, she says she glimpsed the afterlife."

"...My next experience was really lying on the ground outside of the car, and it was actually an out-of-body experience that I had," says Leslie, who declined to give her last name. "I was

actually floating above my body, and I looked down, and I saw all these men working on this poor girl who was down below, about ten feet below me, and she was struggling."

The study reported in *Lancet* looked at 344 patients in the Netherlands who were successfully resuscitated after suffering cardiac arrest in 10 Dutch hospitals.

Rather than using data from people reporting past near-death experiences, researchers talked to patients within a week after they had suffered clinical deaths and been resuscitated. (Clinical death was defined as a period of unconsciousness caused by insufficient blood supply to the brain.)

About 18 percent of the patients in the study reported being able to recall some portion of what happened when they were clinically dead; and 8 to 12 percent reported going through "near-death" experiences, such as seeing lights at the end of tunnels, or being able to speak to dead relatives or friends. Most had excellent recall of the events, which undermines the theory that the memories are false, the study said.

"We don't even begin to have the tools to debate the subject on a rational scientific basis," Johnson told *Good Morning America.* "I don't think our belief on afterlife is defined on a cause of the brain." Johnson, who serves as assisting minister of the Community Covenant Church in West Peabody, Mass., said belief in the afterlife remains primarily a matter of personal faith.

Lead researcher Pim van Lommel of the Hospital Rijnstate in the Netherlands said the study suggests that researchers investigating consciousness should not look in the cells and molecules alone.

Even when the brain is not showing signs of electrical activity, it is possible that a person can still be conscious, he said. In other words, people can be conscious of events around them even when they are physically unconscious.

"Compare it with a TV program," he told *The Washington Post*. "If you open the TV set you will not find the program. The TV set is a receiver. When you turn off your TV set, the program is still there but you can't see it. When you put off your brain, your consciousness is still there but you can't feel it in your body."

Many people describe seeing their own bodies from a distance, as though watching a movie. Others say they felt their bodies rushing toward a brilliant light.

Some who have had this experience say it's a sign there is a tunnel that leads to eternal life, but researchers do not really know what the visions mean. The study does not address whether there is such a thing as the soul, God or the afterlife.

"I think what's happening is that people are trying to validate their experience by making these paranormal claims, but you don't need to do that," said Susan Blackmore, a psychology professor at the University of the West of England in Bristol. "They're valid experiences in themselves, only they're happening in the brain and not in the world out there."

She believes the experiences are like a movie that our brains run at times of extreme traumatic stress. The brain creates endorphins which can reduce pain, and under extreme stress, these large amounts of endorphins produce a dreamlike state of euphoria.

What is Life Beyond Death?

Some of those who described the experiences to ABC NEWS say they feel they were given the opportunity to explore life beyond death.

"I was looking down, and I saw my body, and I saw the doctors," said Jessie Lott, one woman who was resuscitated.

"I had come into this place of brilliant, beautiful life," said another, Dannion Brinkley.

"The feeling of peacefulness, the feeling of utter acceptance, utter I mean, love, and it sounds so hokey, and I hate that part of it, because there aren't really good words to describe it," Leslie said.

Another woman described how she felt she was being pulled toward a giant tunnel, a common theme in the near-death experiences.

"I couldn't stop it. I didn't know why I was moving. I was just pulled right through this enormous, infinite tunnel," said Diane Morrissey.

Blackmore says science can also explain those tunnels: Electrical brain scans show that in our last moments, as the brain is deprived of oxygen, cells fire frantically and at random in the part of the brain which govern vision.

"Now, imagine that you've got lots and lots of cells firing in the middle, towards fewer at the outside, what's it going to look like? Bright light in the middle fading off towards dark at the outside," Blackmore said. "I think that's where the tunnel comes from. And as the oxygen level drops, so the bright light becomes bigger and more immediate, and you get this sensation of rushing forward into the light."

But not all scientists are skeptics when it comes to explaining near-death phenomena, and researchers have debated such issues for years.

Joyce Hawkes, a cell biologist with a Ph.D., had an accident that forever changed her life and her view of science. She suffered a concussion from a falling window.

"I think that part of me that my spirit, my soul left my body and went to another reality," she said. She was surprised at the experience.

"It just was not part of the paradigm in which I lived as a scientist," Hawkes recalled. "It was a big surprise to me to have this sense of something different than the body a consciousness different than the body and to be in this wonderfully healing, peaceful, nurturing place."

Hawkes now works as a spiritual healer.

"I think what I learned was that there truly is no death, that

there is a change in state from a physical form to a spirit form, and that there's nothing to fear about that passage," she said.

The Dutch researchers found that people who had such experiences reported marked changes in their personalities compared with those who had come near death, but had not had those experiences. They seemed to have lost their fear of death, and became more compassionate, loving people.

"I can hardly wait to die, and yet I don't have a death wish. I live my life a hundred percent more now because I have such a fine appreciation about what might happen to us and where we might go," said Morrissey.

Manushya looked at the pamphlet, which had been kept on his chair, when he took his seat. Manushya glanced through the pamphlet.

Near-Death Experiences: In or out of the body?

SUSAN BLACKMORE

Published in Skeptical Inquirer 1991, 16, 34-45

What is it like to die? Although most of us fear death to a greater or lesser extent, there are now more and more people who have "come back" from states close to death and have told stories of usually very pleasant and even joyful experiences at death's door.

For many experiencers, their adventures seem unquestionably to provide evidence for life after death, and the profound effects the experience can have on them is just added confirmation. By contrast, for many scientists these experiences are just hallucinations produced by the dying brain and of no more interest than an especially vivid dream.

So which is right? Are near-death experiences (NDEs) the prelude to our life after death or the very last experience we have before oblivion? I shall argue that neither is quite right: NDEs provide no evidence for life after death, and we can best understand them by looking at neurochemistry, physiology, and psychology; but they are much more interesting than any dream. They seem completely real and can transform people's lives. Any satisfactory theory has to understand that tooand that leads us to questions about minds, selves, and the nature of consciousness.

The seminar continued, the guest spoke:

We now talk of the Deathbed Experiences, toward the end of the last century the physical sciences and the new theory of evolution were making great progress, but many people felt that science was forcing out the traditional ideas of the spirit and soul. Spiritualism began to flourish, and people flocked to mediums to get in contact with their dead friends and relatives "on the other side." Spiritualists claimed, and indeed still claim, to have found proof of survival.

In 1882, the Society for Psychical Research was founded, and serious research on the phenomena began; but convincing evidence for survival is still lacking over one hundred years later (Blackmore 1988). In 1926, a psychical researcher and Fellow of the Royal Society, Sir William Barrett (1926), published a little book on deathbed visions. The dying apparently saw other worlds before they died and even saw and spoke to the dead. There were cases of music heard at the time of death and reports of attendants actually seeing the spirit leave the body.

With modern medical techniques, deathbed visions like these have become far less common. In those days people died at home with little or no medication and surrounded by their family and friends. Today most people die in the hospital and all too often alone. Paradoxically it is also improved medicine that has led to an increase in quite a different kind of report that of the near-death experience.

Resuscitation from ever more serious heart failure has provided accounts of extraordinary experiences (although this is not the only cause of NDEs). These remained largely ignored until about 15 years ago, when Raymond Moody (1975), an American physician, published his best-selling Life After Life. He had talked with many people who had "come back from death," and he put together an account of a typical NDE. In this idealized experience a person hears himself pronounced dead.

Then comes a loud buzzing or ringing noise and a long, dark tunnel. He can see his own body from a distance and watch what is happening. Soon he meets others and a "being of light" who shows him a playback of events from his life and helps him to evaluate it. At some point he gets to a barrier and knows that he has to go back. Even though he feels joy, love, and peace there, he returns to his body and life. Later he tries to tell others; but they don't understand, and he soon gives up. Nevertheless the experience deeply affects him, especially his views about life and death.

Many scientists reacted with disbelief. They assumed Moody was at least exaggerating, but he claimed that no one had noticed the experiences before because the patients were too frightened to talk about them. The matter was soon settled by further research. One cardiologist had talked to more than 2,000 people over a period of nearly 20 years and claimed that more than half reported Moody-type experiences (Schoonmaker 1979). In 1982, a Gallup poll found that about 1 in 7 adult Americans had been close to death and about 1 in 20 had had an NDE. It appeared that Moody, at least in outline, was right. In my own research I have come across numerous reports like this one, sent to me by a woman from Cyprus:

An emergency gastrectomy was performed. On the 4th day following that operation I went into shock and became unconscious for several hours. . . Although thought to be unconscious, I remembered, for years afterwards, the entire, detailed conversation that passed between the surgeon and anesthetist present.... I was lying above my own body, totally free of pain, and looking down at my own self with compassion for the agony I could see on the face; I was floating peacefully Then . . . I was going elsewhere, floating towards a dark, but not frightening, curtain-like area.... Then I felt total peace.

Suddenly it all changedI was slammed back into my body again, very much aware of the agony again.

Within a few years some of the basic questions were being

answered. Kenneth Ring (1980), at the University of Connecticut, surveyed 102 people who had come close to death and found almost 50 percent had had what he called a "core experience." He broke this into five stages: peace, body separation, entering the darkness (which is like the tunnel), seeing the light, and entering the light. He found that the later stages were reached by fewer people, which seems to imply that there is an ordered set of experiences waiting to unfold.

One interesting question is whether NDEs are culture specific. What little research there is suggests that in other cultures NDEs have basically the same structure, although religious background seems to influence the way it is interpreted. A few NDEs have even been recorded in children. It is interesting to note that nowadays children are more likely to see living friends than those who have died, presumably because their playmates only rarely die of diseases like scarlet fever or smallpox.

Perhaps more important is whether you have to be nearly dead to have an NDE. The answer is clearly no (e.g., Morse et al. 1989). Many very similar experiences are recorded of people who have taken certain drugs, were extremely tired, or, occasionally, were just carrying on their ordinary activities.

I must emphasize that these experiences seem completely realeven more real (whatever that may mean) than everyday life. The tunnel experience is not like just imagining going along a tunnel. The view from out of the body seems completely realistic, not like a dream, but as though you really are up there and looking down. Few people experience such profound emotions and insight again during their lifetimes. They do not say, "I've been hallucinating," "I imagined I went to heaven," or "Can I tell you about my lovely dream?" They are more likely to say, "I have been out of my body" or "I saw Grandma in heaven."

Since not everyone who comes close to death has an NDE, it is interesting to ask what sort of people are more likely to have them. Certainly you don't need to be mentally unstable. NDEers do not differ from others in terms of their psychological health or background. Moreover, the NDE does seem to produce profound and positive personality change. After this extraordinary experience people claim that they are no longer so motivated by greed and material achievement but are more concerned about other people and their needs. Any theory of the NDE needs to account for this effect.

Astral Projection and the Next World: Could we have another body that is the vehicle of consciousness and leaves the physical body at death to go on to another world? This, essentially, is the doctrine of astral projection. In various forms it is very popular and appears in a great deal of New Age and occult literature.

One reason may be that out-of-body experiences (OBEs) are quite common, quite apart from their role in NDEs. Surveys have shown that anywhere from 8 percent (in Iceland) to as much as 50 percent (in special groups, such as marijuana users) have had OBEs at some time during their lives. In my own survey of residents of Bristol I found 12 percent. Typically these people had been resting or lying down and suddenly felt they had left their bodies, usually for no more than a minute or two.

A survey of more than 50 different cultures showed that almost all of them believe in a spirit or soul that could leave the body. So both the OBE and the belief in another body are common, but what does this mean? Is it just that we cannot bring ourselves to believe that we are nothing more than a mortal body and that death is the end? Or is there really another body?

You might think that such a theory has no place in science and ought to be ignored. I disagree. The only ideas that science can do nothing with are the purely metaphysical onesideas that have no measurable consequences and no testable predictions. But if a theory makes predictions, however bizarre, then it can be tested.

The theory of astral projection is, at least in some forms, testable. In the earliest experiments mediums claimed they were able to project their astral bodies to distant rooms and see what was happening.

They claimed not to taste bitter aloes on their real tongues, but immediately screwed up their faces in disgust when the substance was placed on their (invisible) astral tongues. Unfortunately these experiments were not properly controlled.

In other experiments, dying people were weighed to try to detect the astral body as it left. Early this century a weight of about one ounce was claimed, but as the apparatus became more sensitive the weight dropped, implying that it was not a real effect. More recent experiments have used sophisticated detectors of ultraviolet and infrared, magnetic flux or field strength, temperature, or weight to try to capture the astral body of someone having an out-of-body experience. They have even used animals and human "detectors," but no one has yet succeeded in detecting anything reliably.

If something really leaves the body in OBEs, then you might expect it to be able to see at a distance. In other words to have extrasensory perception (ESP). There have been several experiments with concealed targets. One success was Tart's subject, who lay on a bed with a five-digit number on a shelf above it (Tart 1968). During the night she had an OBE and correctly reported the number, but critics argued that she could have climbed out of the bed to look. Apart from this one, the experiments tend, like so many in parapsychology, to provide equivocal results and no clear signs of any ESP.

So, this theory has been tested but seems to have failed its tests. If there really were astral bodies I would have expected us to have found something out about them by nowother than how hard it is to track them down!

In addition there are major theoretical objections to the idea of astral bodies. If you imagine that the person has gone to another world, perhaps along some "real" tunnel, then you have to ask what relationship there is between this world and the other one.

If the other world is an extension of the physical, then it ought to be observable and measurable. The astral body, astral world, and tunnel ought to be detectable in some way, and we ought to be able to say where exactly the tunnel is going. The fact that we can't, leads many people to say the astral world is "on another plane," at a "higher level of vibration," and the like. But unless you can specify just what these mean the ideas are completely empty, even though they may sound appealing. Of course we can never prove that astral bodies don't exist, but my guess is that they probably don't and that this theory is not a useful way to understand OBEs.

Another popular theory makes dying analogous with being born: that the out-of-body experience is literally just that reliving the moment when you emerged from your mother's body. The tunnel is the birth canal and the white light is the light of the world into which you were born. Even the being of light can be "explained" as an attendant at the birth.

This theory was proposed by Stanislav Grof and Joan Halifax (1977) and popularized by the astronomer Carl Sagan (1979), but it is pitifully inadequate to explain the NDE. For a start the newborn infant would not see anything like a tunnel as it was being born.

The birth canal is stretched and compressed and the baby usually forced through it with the top of its head, not with its eyes (which are closed anyway) pointing forward. Also it does not have the mental skills to recognize the people around, and these capacities change so much during growing that adults cannot reconstruct what it was like to be an infant.

"Hypnotic regression to past lives" is another popular claim.

In fact much research shows that people who have been hypnotically regressed give the appearance of acting like a baby or a child, but it is no more than acting. For example, they don't make drawings like a real five-year-old would do but like an adult imagines children do. Their vocabulary is too large and in general they overestimate the abilities of children at any given age. There is no evidence (even if the idea made sense) of their "really" going back in time.

Of course the most important question is whether this theory could be tested, and to some extent it can. For example, it predicts that people born by Caesarean section should not have the same tunnel experiences and OBEs. I conducted a survey of people born normally and those born by Caesarean (190 and 36 people, respectively). Almost exactly equal percentages of both groups had had tunnel experiences (36 percent) and OBEs (29 percent). I have not compared the type of birth of people coming close to death, but this would provide further evidence (Blackmore 1982b).

In response to these findings some people have argued that it is not one's own birth that is relived but the idea of birth in general. However, this just reduces the theory to complete vacuousness.

Perhaps we should give up and conclude that all the experiences are "just imagination" or "nothing but hallucinations." However, this is the weakest theory of all. The experiences must, in some sense, be hallucinations, but this is not, on its own, any explanation. We have to ask why are they these kinds of hallucinations? Why tunnels?

Some say the tunnel is a symbolic representation of the gateway to another world. But then why always a tunnel and not, say, a gate, doorway, or even the great River Styx? Why the light at the end of the tunnel? And why always above the body, not below it?

I have no objection to the theory that the experiences are hallucinations. I only object to the idea that you can explain them by saying, "They are just hallucinations." This explains nothing. A viable theory would answer these questions without dismissing the experiences. That, even if only in tentative form, is what I shall try to provide.

Tunnels do not only occur in near death. They are also experienced in epilepsy and migraine, when falling asleep, meditating, or just relaxing, with pressure on both eyeballs, and with certain drugs, such as LSD, psilocybin, and mescaline. It is as though the whole world becomes a rushing, roaring tunnel and you are flying along it toward a bright light at the end. No doubt many readers have also been there, for surveys show that about a third of people havelike this terrified man of 28 who had just had the anesthetic for a circumcision.

In the 1930s, Heinrich Klüver, at the University of Chicago, noted four form constants in hallucinations: the tunnel, the spiral, the lattice or grating, and the cobweb. Their origin probably lies in the structure of the visual cortex, the part of the brain that processes visual information. Imagine that the outside world is mapped onto the back of the eye (on the retina), and then again in the cortex. The mathematics of this mapping (at least to a reasonable approximation) is well known.

Jack Cowan, a neurobiologist at the University of Chicago,

has used this mapping to account for the tunnel. (Cowan 1982). Brain activity is normally kept stable by some cells inhibiting others. Disinhibition (the reduction of this inhibitory activity) produces too much activity in the brain. This can occur near death (because of lack of oxygen) or with drugs like LSD, which interfere with inhibition. Cowan uses an analogy with fluid mechanics to argue that disinhibition will induce stripes of activity that move across the cortex. Using the mapping it can easily be shown that stripes in the cortex would appear like concentric rings or spirals in the visual world. In other words, if you have stripes in the cortex you will seem to see a tunnel-like pattern of spirals or rings.

This theory is important in showing how the structure of the brain could produce the same hallucination for everyone. The most obvious thing about the representation in the cortex is that there are lots of cells representing the center of the visual field but very few for the edges. This means that you can see small things very clearly in the center, but if they are out at the edges you cannot.

The computer program starts with thinly spread dots of light, mapped in the same way as the cortex, with more toward the middle and very few at the edges. Gradually the number of dots increases, mimicking the increasing noise. Now the center begins to look like a white blob and the outer edges gradually get more and more dots. And so it expands until eventually the whole screen is filled with light. The appearance is just like a dark speckly tunnel with a white light at the end, and the light grows bigger and bigger (or nearer and nearer) until it fills the whole screen.

If it seems odd that such a simple picture can give the impression that you are moving, consider two points. First, it is known that random movements in the periphery of the visual field are more likely to be interpreted by the brain as outward than inward movements.

Second, the brain infers our own movement to a great extent from what we see. Therefore, presented with an apparently growing patch of flickering white light your brain will easily interpret it as yourself moving forward into a tunnel.

The theory also makes a prediction about NDEs in the blind. If they are blind because of problems in the eye but have a normal cortex, then they too should see tunnels. But if their blindness stems from a faulty or damaged cortex, they should not. These predictions have yet to be tested.

According to this kind of theory there is, of course, no real tunnel. Nevertheless there is a real physical cause of the tunnel experience. It is noise in the visual cortex. This way we can explain the origin of the tunnel without just dismissing the experiences and without needing to invent other bodies or other worlds.

Like tunnels, OBEs are not confined to near death. They too can occur when just relaxing and falling asleep, with meditation, and in epilepsy and migraine. They can also, at least by a few people, be induced at will.

It is important to remember that these experiences seem quite real. People don't describe them as dreams or fantasies but as events that actually happened.

However, we have seen how poorly the astral projection and birth theories cope with OBEs. What we need is a theory that involves no immeasurable entities or untestable other worlds but explains why the experiences happen; and why they seem so real.

I would start by asking why anything seems real. You might think this is obviousafter all, the things we see out there are real aren't they? Well no, in a sense they aren't. As perceiving creatures all we know is what our senses tell us. And our senses tell us what is "out there" by constructing models of the world with ourselves in it. The whole of the world "out there" and our own.

Bodies are really constructions of our minds. Yet we are sure, all the time, that this constructionif you like, this "model of reality"is "real" while the other fleeting thoughts we have are unreal. We call the rest of them daydreams, imagination, fantasies, and so on. Our brains have no trouble distinguishing "reality" from "imagination." But this distinction is not given. It is one the brain has to make for itself by deciding which of its own models represents the world "out there." I suggest it does this by comparing all the models it has at any time and choosing the most stable one as "reality."

This will normally work very well. The model created by the senses is the best and most stable the system has. It is obviously "reality," while that image I have of the bar I'm going to go to later is unstable and brief.

The choice is easy. By comparison, when you are almost asleep, very frightened, or nearly dying, the model from the senses will be confused and unstable. If you are under terrible stress or suffering oxygen deprivation, then the choice won't be so easy. All the models will be unstable.

So what will happen now? Possibly the tunnel being created by noise in the visual cortex will be the most stable model and so, according to my supposition, this will seem real. Fantasies and imagery might become more stable than the sensory model, and so seem real. The system will have lost input control.

What then should a sensible biological system do to get back to normal? I would suggest that it could try to ask itselfas it were"Where am I? What is happening?" Even a person under severe stress will have some memory left. They might recall the accident, or know that they were in hospital for an operation, or remember the pain of the heart attack. So they will try to reconstruct, from what little they can remember, what is happening.

Now we know something very interesting about memory models. Often they are constructed in a bird's-eye view. That is, the events or scenes are seen as though from above. If you find this strange, try to remember the last time you went to a pub or the last time you walked along the seashore. Where are "you" looking from in this recalled scene? If you are looking from above you will see what I mean.

So te explanation of the OBE becomes clear. A memory

model in bird's-eye view has taken over from the sensory model. It seems perfectly real because it is the best model the system has got at the time. Indeed, it seems real for just the same reason anything ever seems real.

This theory of the OBE leads to many testable predictions, for example, that people who habitually use bird's-eye views should be more likely to have OBEs.

Both Harvey Irwin (1986), an Australian psychologist, and myself (Blackmore 1987) have found that people who dream as though they were spectators have more OBEs, although there seems to be no difference for the waking use of different viewpoints.

Of course this theory says that the OBE world is only a memory model. It should only match the real world when the person has already known about something or can deduce it from available information. This presents a big challenge for research on near death.

Some researchers claim that people near death can actually see things that they couldn't possibly have known about. For example, the American cardiologist Michael Sabom (1982) claims that patients reported the exact behavior of needles on monitoring apparatus when they had their eyes closed and appeared to be unconscious. Further, he compared these descriptions with those of people imagining they were being resuscitated and found that the real patients gave far more accurate and detailed descriptions.

There are problems with this comparison. Most important,

the people really being resuscitated could probably feel some of the manipulations being done on them and hear what was going on. Hearing is the last sense to be lost and, as you will realize if you ever listen to radio plays or news, you can imagine a very clear visual image when you can only hear something. So the dying person could build up a fairly accurate picture this way.

The experience of seeing excerpts from your life flash before you is not really as mysterious as it first seems. It has long been known that stimulation of cells in the temporal lobe of the brain can produce instant experiences that seem like the reliving of memories. Also, temporal-lobe epilepsy can produce similar experiences, and such seizures can involve other limbic structures in the brain, such as the amygdala and hippocampus, which are also associated with memory.

Imagine that the noise in the dying brain stimulates cells like this. The memories will be aroused and, according to my hypothesis, if they are the most stable model the system has at that time they will seem real. For the dying person they may well be more stable than the confused and noisy sensory model.

The link between temporal-lobe epilepsy and the NDE has formed the basis of a thorough neurobiological model of the NDE. They suggest that the brain stress consequent on the near-death episode leads to the release of neuropeptides and neurotransmitters (in particular the endogenous endorphins). These then stimulate the limbic system and other connected areas. In addition, the effect of the endorphins could account the blissful and other positive emotional states so often associated with the NDE.

Of course there is more to the review than just memories. The person feels as though she or he is judging these life events, being shown their significance and meaning. But this too, I suggest, is not so very strange. When the normal world of the senses is gone and memories seem real, our perspective on our life changes. We can no longer be attached to our plans, hopes, ambitions, and fears, which fade away and become unimportant, while the past comes to life again. We can only accept it as it is, and there is no one to judge it but ourselves.

Now we come to what might seem the most extraordinary parts of the NDE; the worlds beyond the tunnel and OBE. But I think you can now see that they are not so extraordinary at all. In this state the outside world is no longer real, and inner worlds are. Whatever we can imagine clearly enough will seem real. And what will we imagine when we know we are dying? I am sure for many people it is the world they expect or hope to see. Their minds may turn to people they have known who have died before them or to the world they hope to enter next. Like the other images we have been considering, these will seem perfectly real.

Finally, there are those aspects of the NDE that are ineffable—they cannot be put into words. I suspect that this is because some people take yet another step, a step into nonbeing.

I shall try to explain this by asking another question. What is consciousness? If you say it is a thing, another body, a substance, you will only get into the kinds of difficulty we got into with OBEs. I prefer to say that consciousness is just what it is like being a mental model. In other words, all the mental models in any person's mind are all conscious, but only one is a model of "me." This is the one that I think of as myself and to which I relate everything else. It gives a core to my life. It allows me to think that I am a person, something that lives on all the time. It allows me to ignore the fact that "I" change from moment to moment and even disappear every night in sleep.

Now when the brain comes close to death, this model of self may simply fall apart. Now there is no self. It is a strange and dramatic experience. For there is no longer an experienceryet there is experience.

This state is obviously hard to describe, for the "you" who is trying to describe it cannot imagine not being. Yet this profound experience leaves its mark. The self never seems quite the same again.

I think we can now see why an essentially physiological event can change people's lives so profoundly. The experience has jolted their usual (and erroneous) view of the relationship between themselves and the world. We all too easily assume that we are some kind of persistent entity inhabiting a perishable body. But, as the Buddha taught we have to see through that illusion. The world is only a construction of an information-processing system, and the self is too. I believe that the NDE gives people a glimpse into the nature of their own minds that is hard to get any other way.

Drugs can produce it temporarily, mystical experiences can do it for rare people, and long years of practice in meditation or mindfulness can do it. But the NDE can out of the blue strike anyone and show them what they never knew before, that their body is only that a lump of fleshthat they are not so very important after all. And that is a very freeing and enlightening experience.

If my analysis of the NDE is correct, we can extrapolate to the next stage. Lack of oxygen first produces increased activity through disinhibition, but eventually it all stops. Since it is this activity that produces the mental models that give rise to consciousness, then all this will cease. There will be no more experience, no more self, and so that, as far as my constructed self is concerned, is the end.

So, are NDEs in or out of the body? I should say neither, for neither experiences nor selves have any location. It is finally death that dissolves the illusion that we are a solid self inside a body.

Manushya grasped everything. N.D.E. was a look into death, a fleeting moment. But, what about Dying and the actual death. What happens after death? In N.D.E. you saw tunnels, you had an O.B.E. But, what about death? What happens after death?

Manushya started buying books, attending seminars, visiting Mahatmas, Rishis, Sages and summarized death as follows:

In connection with a description of the passage of the soul after the death of the body, we are introduced into a new subject, that of the existence of certain psychic nerve currents inside us, known as the *nadis.* There are certain *nadis* in our bodies which exist very subtly in the astral layer of our personality and control not only the entire physiological system but also our minds and breathing process, the entire personality. Those who are versed in the science of *hatha-yoga* will know very well the importance of these *nadis*.

These nerve currents are supposed to be filled with certain subtle juices which are referred to here as *animna,* very slight extradition which controls the humors of the body. The point that the Upanishad makes out particularly here is that there is a tremendous connection between the sun and these nerves.

It is not that the sun is spatially very far from us. We have a false notion that the stars in the heaven and the sun in the sky are very far and that they have no connection at all with us here on earth. This intervening space, which is the apparent cause for this seeming disconnection is not empty. It is a vital fluid. The ordinary physical notion of the commonplace astronomers that space is not organically connected with the individual has to be given up. In fact, higher aspects of astronomy going into the realm of astrology will tell us that space is not a disconnecting element. If it is, there would be no influence of the planets upon us. They exert a tremendous influence, not merely in a mechanical manner as the law of gravitation does, but in a very, very living and organic manner.

This subtle substance in the nerve currents is of different colours. It may be brownish-yellow, or white, or blue, or yellow proper, or red. These are the types specially mentioned here, though there can be many other permutations and combinations of these colours because we cannot actually count the number of these nerve currents in the system.

There are several thousands of *nadis,* but the principal among them are hundred and one in number. It is believed from the standpoint of this section of the Upanishad that the colours of these nerve currents inside us are due to the influence of the sun upon us.

Variegated influences are exerted upon us in respect of the constitution of our personality by the rays of the sun. Even after the sun sets at night, it continues to influence us. The influence of the sun does not cease merely because it is midnight. It is a tremendous influence exerted upon the whole earth. Night and day make no difference for this. When the effect of the sun through its rays has an impact upon the bile in our system, these juices become brownish yellow in colour. When there is phlegmatic element mixed with this bile, it is supposed to be whitish in colour. When the wind element also is included within it, that means to say when the wind humor is a little more predominant, it assumes a blue colour. When there is an equal distribution of the phlegmatic matter and the bile element it becomes yellow, while the reddish element is due to the preponderance of the red corpuscles in the blood influencing these juices in the system.

Now, the idea is that the colours of these juices in the nerves are imported, as it were, from the colours in the sun. They are the reflections, as it were, of the sun's rays experienced by us through our own nervous system. So the Upanishad says that these colours are in the sun and they are in the *nadis*. But what about the causes thereof? These colours,brownish yellow, or white, or blue, or actual yellow, or redare the colours of the sun's internal structure. We know the sun's rays have colours, and these are responsible for the colours of the juices which flow in the nerve currents.

Just as a national highway passing through villages connects one section of villages on one side to another section on the other side, even so the sun's rays seem to be traveling throughout space like highways, as it were, emanating from the sun, touching the heavens on one side and influencing the individuals and the whole earth on the other side. These rays of the sun are like passages or highways in the entire space. They touch this world and also the other world. They enter even the minutest thing in this world, like X-rays penetrating through objects, and we are not excluded from the influence of these subtle rays of the sun. They penetrate through the nerves inside us, they get refracted back into space and return to the sun, so that they convey a message to the sun, as it were, as to what our predicament is here.

Thus we see there is a real living connection between the sun and ourselves here. The rays are like messengers coming from the sun, conveying to us the message from the sun and taking our message from here and conveying it back to the sun, like postmen. This kind of work the rays of the sun perform much more effectively and vitally than the postal department does!

The sun there and ourselves here belong to one family, an undivided family. So, we are like brothers. Most undivided families have division among the members and the undividedness is only an imagination. Really the members of the family are divided. But here the connection is not mere imagination. It is a real interconnection of vital forces in us with the sun and with everything between the sun and ourselves.

So we can imagine what integral connection we have really with the atmosphere and the heavens and the stellar system, in spite of our apparently being here as if separated and disconnected. This disconnection is a misconception in our minds.

It is these nerve currents that are responsible for the withdrawal of the mind into itself in deep sleep. What we call deep sleep, the composure of the mind, the withdrawal of the mind from all sense activity and the retiring from all dream experience also, where one knows nothing,that experience is brought about by the travel of the various rays of the mind through these nerve currents to the centre of the heart.

There the mind then lies sleeping and inactive, doing nothing and knowing nothing. So these *nadis* have some part to play even in the activity called psychic sleep. In the state of deep sleep we are overpowered by a supernal light.

There are various opinions as to what happens in deep sleep. They differ one from the other. One of the theories is that we fall asleep on account of the fatigue of the senses which results in the exhaustion of the mind searching for happiness in the world. The other doctrine is that the bilious element in our system gets roused up due to the activity of the sun's rays during the day and they make us fatigued in a different way altogether, compelling us to fall asleep.

The third theory is that when the mind goes back to its source, it is overwhelmed by the light of the Atman. This getting blinded by that light is in a way equal to seeing nothing. It is seeing darkness, as it were, as perhaps when we gaze at the sun for a long time we see not the brilliance of the sun any more but only pitch darkness. This is a very mystical doctrine of sleep which tells us that we are confronted by the brilliance of the Atman when we go to sleep.

And, therefore, on account of there being nothing to see, objectiveness being withdrawn completely, we fall into a mood of so-called unconsciousness, merely because there is nothing for the senses to do and there is nothing for the mind to think. So when there is nothing to sense and nothing to think, what is our condition? It is a falling back into an oblivion of all kinds of experiences.

Now we are introduced to the principal subject of this section. The other points mentioned in connection with these nerves are introductory to the main point, which is the theme of the section, namely the departure of the soul after death.

When a person becomes weak due to old age and is awaiting impending death, people get anxious about his condition. They sit round him thinking that he is about to leave this world. And then they query, "Do you recognize us?", "Do you know I am your father?", "I am so-and-so related to you, do you recognize me?", "Do you know I am your son?", and so on. He is able to reply to these people in a sensible manner as long as the *pranas* do not depart from the body and as long as the mind is capable of working in a normal fashion in respect of the body. But when the mind is compelled by the *pranas* to withdraw itself into its source, no sensation, no thought, no recognition remains whatsoever. Then what happens to that person?

The very same rays of the sun, about which we have discussed earlier in this section, with which we have such an intimate connection, become the passage of the soul for its ascent into the higher regions. These rays of the sun are the roads or the paths, as it were, for the soul when it rises upwards after the departure from this body.

This description is in connection with the death of a purified person who is expected to attain liberation by progressive stages, called by the name *kramamukti,* gradual liberation. Such a person chants Om at the time of death. Everyone will not chant Om at this crucial moment. Those who are accustomed to such a practice throughout life, who have led a very disciplined life of spiritual contemplation throughout their career on earth, will be able to recollect this practice at the time of passing, when usually the mind gets confounded due to the action of natural forces.

How much time does the soul take to jump into the sun? It takcs as much timc as thc mind will takc to go to any place. That means it does not take much time. The so-called distance of 93 million miles between the sun up there and the individual here on this earth makes no difference to the soul. It does not take any time at all to reach the sun. Such is the quickness of its action. The soul is taken to the sun at such speed through the passage of the rays. The moment it thinks, it is there. So quickly it is taken there.

This sun is the glorious passage to *Brahma-loka,* the realm of the Creator. This is the entrance to the glorious immortal abode of Brahma. And also it is the halting and checking place, as it were, for the unknowing persons. Those who do not carry an 'accepted passport' are turned back from the sun. Everyone cannot go there. The knowers go there and the unknowers return. The latter will not even be allowed to touch that spot. So the sun is the check-post where there is a filtering of souls, as it were. The purified ones are allowed to go beyond and the unpurified ones are kicked back to the earth. He is an entrance to the region of Brahma to the purified ones and also a closed door to those who are unprepared for this ascent.

In this connection there is a verse, says the Upanishad.

Tad esa slokah:

satam caika ca hrdayasya nadyah
tasam murdhanam abhinihsrtaika,
tayordhvam ayan amrtatvam eti
visvannya utkramane bhavanti,
utkramane bhavanti.

One hundred and one are the principal nerve currents in this body. One among these hundred and one moves vertically, as it were, towards the crown of the head. This is usually called the *sushumna-nadi* in Yogic language. If our *prana* and minds can travel through this central nerve current called the *sushumna* and up through the crown of the head, we attain immortality. And this is *kramamukti,* gradual liberation.

But if the *pranas* depart not by this central nerve through the crown of the head but through other orifices in the body, then there is rebirth. It may be in this world or it may be in some other lower world, according to the particular passage which the *pranas* seek at the time of exit. No liberation is possible unless the movement is through *sushumna-nadi.* So here one part of the discussion of this important subject of the Atman in the heart is concluded.

Now, what happens after death? The soft body with the Atma also known as Preta is said to be of six types. In LOKAS Sri Swami Sivananda explains the Yoga Vasishtha by Sage Vasishtha:

"The Pretas are of six kinds, namely,

? the slightly sinful,
? the ordinarily sinful,
? the greatly sinful,
? the slightly virtuous,
? the ordinarily virtuous,
? and the greatly virtuous.

Some of the most sinful Pretas continue to be experiencing the insensibility of death like a stone for a period of a year. Regaining awareness they experience that they are doomed to suffer from the endless torments of hell which their Vasanas have brought them, for a long time. They then undergo the experience of hundreds of incarnations until they finally get rid of the experience of world-illusion, by finding peace within.

There are others in this class, who, after their inactivity of death is over, begin to experience the unutterable pain of insensibility in the form of immovable trees, etc. Then they undergo the torments of hell, after which they are again born on earth in accordance with their earthly desires.

✍ *Those of ordinary sin* experience the inertness of stone for some time after death. Being awakened to consciousness, they, then or after some time, undergo the experience of the lives of birds, reptiles or beasts, before they turn to their usual lives in the world.

✍ *The slightly sinful* souls, often immediately after the insensibility of death, come to assume some human form to continue their earthly existence in accordance with their previous desires. They come to the worldly consciousness soon after their death and their previous desires and imagination evolve new worlds in their experience in a dream-like manner.

✍ *The greatly virtuous* souls, soon after the insensibility of death is over, get an experience in the worlds of gods. Having enjoyed the fruits of their virtues in godly personality and in heavenly worlds, they are again born in this world in noble and rich families.

✍ *The souls of ordinary virtuous* experience, after the insensibility of death is over, that they are being carried away by winds and later on are turned into the lives of plants and herbs. Having undergone this experience for some time they feel that they are entering human bodies as food, and there they are turned into spermatozoa and thence enter the wombs of (expectant) mothers."

Thus re-birth takes place after death. Manushaya understood.

"Are there any practices or religious ceremonies to be performed once the person is dead?" Manushya asked a Tibetan monk. The monk explained thus:

"Death, we will remember, is one of the 4 sights that Gautama Shakyamuni is said to have experienced that moved him to pursue an end to suffering for all beings.

It can help us to remember that we have each been wandering in samsara for endless eons, or we can become caught up in the grief of losing our connection with someone which reinforces the belief that this life is all there is. Nevertheless, it is always sad to say goodbye. That sadness can be considered a tribute to the life of the person who has died. Sometimes, it is a reflection of our own regrets.

To dwell on grief though, is not helpful. Instead of focusing on that emotion we can work to end the suffering of our friend, and also of all the other beings wandering in the *bardo* and in samsara.

P'howa

The practice that is done at the time of dying is called *phowa* or *powa* in Tibetan, meaning "transforming." That is, the consciousness is transformed by being ejected from the dying body, to be liberated and eventually, received or transferred to another form of existence.

There are 4 ways to accomplish this transformation, through the Dharmakaya, the Sambhogakaya, the Nirmanakaya or through the forceful method known as *chetsab.*

Generally it is a lama that does the powa, or someone who has received the initiation and is accomplished in the Amitabha practice and who has accumulated 666,000 mantras of that deity.

The Tibetan monk replied: I will tell you of the Teachings of The First Dalai Lama:

"There are three causes of death, namely,

- exhaustion of life span,
- exhaustion of positive energy, and
- exhaustion of karmic life supports.

Each of these has its own remedy. When the death indicated [by knowing the signs of death] has its cause in one or two of the above reasons it can be turned away by the appropriate methods. However, when it is caused by an exhaustion of all three, there is no way to deter the advent of death. All one can do then is to prepare one's mind for death by means of training in the consciousness transference yogas."

When we are experiencing a period of insufficient sustaining energy, longevity practices are one way of improving the situation. Some deities associated with long life are Amitayus, Tara and Usnishavijaya. There is also a yoga called "taking the sky as food."

The First Dalai Lama said on the remedies for the causes of untimely death:

- ✍ Exhaustion of life span -- take long life initiations, practice healing meditations, etc.
- ✍ Exhaustion of merit -- perform tantric feasts and prayers, seek the blessings of holy people, etc.
- ✍ Exhaustion of [sustaining] karma -- purify the mind of negative karmic stains through consciously examining negativity, generating a distaste for negativity, meditation upon love and compassion, or upon the void nature of negativity, etc.

A summary of a simplified practice done at the time of dying:

"Visualize a vivid presence of God, whatever form of God you feel connection with -- Holy Spirit, Jesus, Mary, Buddhas, a pure light, whatever is real to you. Fill your heart with this presence and trust it. Then pray a *p'howa* prayer with the full focus of the heart, mind, and soul.

Through your blessing, grace, and guidance, through the power of the light that streams from you: May all my negative karma, destructive emotions, obscurations, and blockages be purified and removed, May I know myself forgiven for all the harm I may have thought and done, May I accomplish this profound practice of *phowa*, and die a good and peaceful death, and through the triumph of my death, may I be able to benefit all other beings, living or dead.

After this prayer, imagine the presence you have invoked is so moved that he or she responds with pure love and streams of light. The light is completely purifying and healing, and you dissolve completely into the light."

The Buddha's last words are reputed to be, "All things which are made of parts eventually come apart. Be mindful, and achieve the Awakened state!"

Sushumna is the key point of liberation.

One who can enter sushumna at the time of death can attain Brahman, the highest goal of life. All other paths are paths of rebirths.

To leave the body, the yogi awakens the sleeping serpent power of kundalini and this energy enters into the path of sushumna. It rises to the ajna chakra, the two-petalled lotus between the eyebrows. Here the yogi gathers together and controls all the other life force energies of the body, known as pranas. He withdraws his consciousness from earth-bound existence and from the senses, and from the five lower chakras. He concentrates on the ajna chakra and then gradually upward toward sahasrara, the crown chakra. While concentrating on the crown chakra, he leaves the body through the fontanelle and rises finally to the realm of the absolute Brahman.

So, at time of death the soul discards the body, its outer garment. Yama told Nachiketa that after the body is dead and destroyed, the soul continues to exist.

When the soul departs from the body, the subconscious mind goes with it, leaving the gross body behind. The subconscious mind, which is a storehouse of merits and demerits, becomes the vehicle for the jiva, the soul. All the samskaras of our many lives remain in the storehouse of our subconscious mind in a latent state like seeds. The relationship between the subtle body and the gross body is akin to that of the seed and the plant. As the seed contains all the qualities of the plant in the seed germ, so the subconscious mind retains all the samskaras of our previous lives.

Life and death are only different names for the same fact -- the two sides of one coin. One who goes beyond such differentiations can conquer death and reach the other shore, that is, eternal life. A person who understands the fundamental truth that soul, the Atman, the Self is immortal and all else is perishable, can solve the mystery of death *Life after death, can be experienced here, in this very life, by those who have attained samadhi.* Those who have realized their real Self are immortal.

"Then" Manushya asked, perplexed, how do we extend our life?"

"YOGA" was the word spoken by the Monk.

"""PRANAYAMA" "NADI SHUDDI" and dozens of other exercises, cleanses and energises the PRANA inside the body, controls the mind."""" Said the Monk.
"Can you give me a list of these exercises?" asked Manushaya.

The Monk smiled and gave Manushaya the list.The list with definations of postures:

What Is Prana?

Prana is the sum total of all energy that is manifested in the universe. It is the vital force, Sukshma. Breath is the external manifestation of Prana. By exercising control over this gross breath, you can control the subtle Prana inside. Control of Prana means control of mind. Mind cannot operate without the help of Prana. It is the Sukshma Prana that is intimately connected with the mind. Prana is the sum total of all latent forces which are hidden in men and which lie everywhere around us. Heat, light, electricity, magnetism are all the manifestations of Prana. Prana is related to mind; through mind to the will; through will to the individual soul, and through this to the Supreme Being.

The seat of Prana is the heart. Prana is one; but it has many functions to do. Hence it assumes five names according to the different functions it performs, viz., Prana, Apana, Samana, Udana and Vyana. According to the different functions they perform, they occupy certain places in the body.

Breath directed by thought under the control of the will is a vitalising, regenerated force which can be utilized consciously for self-development, for healing many incurable diseases and for many other useful purposes. Hatha Yogins consider that Prana Tattva is superior to Manas Tattva (mind), as Prana is present even when mind is absent during deep sleep. Hence Prana plays a more vital part than mind.

If you know how to control the little waves of Prana working through mind, then the secret of subjugating the universal Prana will be known to you. The Yogin who becomes an expert in the knowledge of this secret, will have no fear from any power, because he has mastery over all manifestations of power in the Universe. What is commonly known, as Power of Personality is nothing more than the natural capacity of a person to wield his Prana. Some people are more powerful in life, more influential and fascinating than others. It is all through this Prana, which the Yogin uses consciously by the command of his will.

Having acquired a thorough knowledge of the seat of Nadis and of the Vayus with their functions, one should begin with the purification of Nadis. A person possessed of Yama and Niyama, avoiding all company, having finished his course of study, delighting in Truth and virtues, having conquered his anger, being engaged in the service of his spiritual instructor and well instructed in all the religious practices, should go to a secluded place for Yoga Abhyasa.

Nadi Suddhi (purification of Nadis) is an important matter in the early stage of Yoga. If there are impurities in the Nadis, the ascent of Kundalini in the Sushumna is seriously retarded. Purity in the Nadis facilitates the ascent of Kundalini. Pranayama brings about quick purification of the Nadis. Nadi Suddhi is the basis of Yoga. It is the foundation of Yoga. It is the first part of Yoga.

Just as you can stop all the other wheels of the factory if you can stop the important fly-wheel of the engine, so also if you can stop the functions of all other organs of the body, you can get control of the subtle, psychic Prana by restraining the breath. That is the reason why Pranayama is prescribed for controlling Prana.

Prana is the over-coat of the mind. If you can control Prana, you can control mind and Veerya also, because Prana, Veerya and mind are under one Sambandha. If you can control mind, breath stops by itself. Prana comes under control. Just as you have a nervous system in the gross physical body, so also there is a nervous system in the astral body. The nervous system of the physical body is the Sthula Prana. The nervous system of the astral body is the Sukshma Prana. There is intimate connection between these two Pranas. There is inter-action between these two Pranas.

By controlling the act of breathing, you can efficiently control all the various functions in the body. You can very easily and quickly control and develop the body, mind and soul.

Psychic cure, Telepathy, Television, thought reading and other Siddhis are the effects of the control of Prana. The process by which the Prana is controlled by regulation of breath is termed 'Pranayama'. It is through Pranayama that you can control your circumstances and character and consciously harmonies the universal individual life with the cosmic life.

To suit the different constitutions, temperament and purpose, in Pranayama there are many varieties of exercises, viz., deep breathing exercise, Sukha Purvaka (easy comfortable) Pranayama during walking, Pranayama during meditation, Rhythmical breathing, Suryabheda, Ujjayi, Sitkari, Sitali, Bhastrika, Bhramari, Murchha, Plavini, Kevala Kumbhaka, etc. Of all the above exercises only the last eight are described in the

Hatha Yogic texts.

Before commencing the practice of Pranayama however, you should clean the Nadis. Then only will you derive the maximum benefit from Pranayama. The cleansing of the Nadi (Nadi-Suddhi) is either Samanu or Nirmanuthat is, with or without the use of Bija. According to the first form, the Yogi in Padmasana or Siddhasana offers his prayers to the Guru and meditates on him. Meditating on 'Yang' (y:□)he does Japa through Ida of the Bija 16 times, Kumbhaka with Japa of the Bija 64 times, and then exhalation through the solar Nadi and Japa of Bija 32 times. Fire is raised from Manipura and united with Prithvi. Then follows inhalation by the solar Nadi with the Vahni Bija 'Rang' (r□)16 times, Kumbhaka with Japa of the Bija 64 times, followed by exhalation through the lunar Nadi and Japa of the Bija 32 times. He then meditates on the lunar brilliance, gazing at the tip of the nose, and inhales by Ida with Japa of the Bija 'Thang' (Y□)16 times. Kumbhaka is done with the Bija 'Vang' (v:□)64 times. He thinks himself as flooded by nectar, and considers that the Nadis have been washed. He exhales by Pingala with Japa of the Bija 'Lang' (l:□) 32 times and considers himself thereby as strengthened. Now I will tell you a few important exercises only, that are useful in awakening the Kundalini.

1. Sukha Purvaka (Easy Comfortable Pranayama)

Sit in Padmasana or Siddhasana. Close the right nostril with your right thumb. Inhale (Puraka) through the left nostril till you count 3 Oms slowly. Imagine that you are drawing the Prana along with the atmospheric air. In course of practice, you will actually feel that you are drawing Prana. Then close the left nostril also with the little and ring fingers of your right hand. Retain the breath till you count 12 Oms. Send the current down to the Muladhara Chakra. Feel that the nerve-current is striking against the Muladhara Chakra and awakening Kundalini. Remove the right thumb and exhale through the right nostril till you count 6 Oms. Again inhale through the right nostril, retain and exhale through the left nostril as stated above. All the above six processes constitute one Pranayama. To start with do 6 Pranayamas in the morning and 6 in the evening. Gradually increase it to 20 Pranayamas for each sitting. The ratio of inhalation, retention and exhalation is 1:4:2. You should gradually increase the period of Kumbhaka.

Be careful in doing the Kumbhaka as long as you can comfortably do. Do not be in a hurry. Be patient. Contract the anus and do Mula Bandha also. Concentrate on the Chakra and meditate on Kundalini. This is the most important portion of this exercise. In this Pranayama, deep concentration plays a vital part in awakening Kundalini. Kundalini will be awakened quickly if the degree of concentration is intense and if practiced regularly.

This exercise removes all diseases, purifies the Nadis, steadies the wandering mind, improves digestion and circulation, helps Brahmacharya, and awakens Kundalini. All the impurities of the body are thrown out.

2. Bhastrika

Rapid succession of forcible expulsions is a characteristic feature of this exercise. 'Bhastrika' means 'bellows' in Sanskrit.

Just as a blacksmith blows his bellows rapidly, so also you should inhale and exhale rapidly. Sit in your favourite Asana. Close the mouth. Inhale and exhale quickly 20 times like the bellows. Constantly dilate and contract the chest as you inhale and exhale. When you practise the Pranayama a hissing sound is produced. You should start with forcible expulsions of breath following one another in rapid succession. After 20 such expulsions, make a deep inhalation and retain the breath as long as you can comfortably do and then slowly exhale. This is one round of Bhastrika.

Begin with 10 expulsions for a round and increase it gradually to 20 or 25 for a round. The period of Kumbhaka also should be gradually and cautiously increased. Rest a while after one round is over and again begin the next round. Do 3 rounds in the beginning and after due practice, do 20 rounds in the morning and 20 in the evening.

Advanced students do this Pranayama after partial closing of the glottis. They do not make a powerful noise like the beginners. They can do it even in a standing posture.

Bhastrika removes inflammation of the throat, increases the gastric fire, destroys phlegm and all diseases of the nose and lungs, eradicates Asthma, consumption and other diseases which arise from the excess of wind, bile and phlegm. It gives warmth to the body. It is the most effective of all Pranayama exercises. It enables Prana to break through the three Granthis. All the other benefits of Sukha Purvaka Pranayama are obtained in this exercise also.

3. Suryabheda

Sit on Padmasana or Siddhasana. Close the eyes. Keep the left nostril closed with your right ring and little fingers. Slowly inhale without making any sound as long as you can do it comfortably through the right nostril. Then close the right nostril with your right thumb and retain the breath by firmly pressing the chin against the chest (Jalandhara Bandha). Hold the breath till perspiration oozes from the roots of the hair (hair follicles). This point cannot be reached at the very outset. You will have to increase the period of Kumbhaka gradually. This is the limit of the sphere of practice of Suryabheda Kumbhaka. Release the Jalandhara Bandha. Then exhale very slowly without making any sound through the left nostril with the thumb closing the right nostril.

"The practice of Suryabheda Kumbhaka destroys decay and death and awakens Kundalini."

This Pranayama should again and again be performed, as it purifies the brain and destroys the intestinal worms. It removes the four kinds of evils caused by Vayu and cures Vata (rheumatism). It cures rhinitis and various sorts of neuralgia. The worms that are found in the frontal sinuses are also destroyed.

4. Ujjayi

Sit in your usual Asana. Close the mouth. Inhale slowly through both the nostrils in a smooth, uniform manner.

Retain the breath as long as you can do it comfortably and

then exhale slowly through the left nostril by closing the right nostril with your right thumb. Expand the chest when you inhale. During inhalation a peculiar sound is produced owing to the partial closing of glottis. The sound produced during inhalation should be of a mild and uniform pitch. It should be continuous also. This Kumbhaka may be practiced even when walking or standing. Instead of exhaling through the left nostril, you can exhale slowly through both nostrils.

This removes the heat in the head. The practitioner becomes very beautiful. The gastric fire is increased. It removes phlegm in the throat. Asthma, consumption and all sorts of pulmonary diseases are cured. All diseases that arise from deficient inhalation of oxygen and diseases of the heart are cured. All works are accomplished by Ujjayi Pranayama. The practitioner is never attacked by diseases of phlegm, nerves, enlargement of spleen, dyspepsia, dysentery, consumption, cough or fever. Perform Ujjayi to destroy decay and death.

5. Plavini

Practice of this Pranayama demands skill on the part of the students. He who practices this Plavini can do Jalastambha and float on water for any length of time, Mr.'S', a Yogic student, can float on water for twelve hours at a stretch. He who practices this Plavini Kumbhaka can live on air and dispense with food for some days. The student actually drinks air slowly like water and sends it to the stomach. The stomach gets bloated a bit. If you tap the stomach when it is filled with air, you will get a peculiar tympanic (air) sound. Gradual practice is necessary. The help of one who is well versed in this Pranayama, is necessary. The student can fill up the stomach with air by gradual belching. After the practice, the air should be completely taken out. It is done by Uddiyana Bandha and hiccough.

6. Pranic Healing

Those who practise Pranayama, can impart their Prana for healing morbid diseases. They can also recharge themselves with Prana in no time by Practising Kumbhaka. Never think that you will be depleted of your Prana by distributing it to others. The more you will give, the more it will flow to you from the cosmic source (Hiranyagarbha). That is the law of Nature. Do not become a niggard. If there is a rheumatic patient, gently shampoo his legs with your hands. When you do shampooing (massage), do Kumbhaka and imagine that the Prana is flowing from your hands towards your patient.

Connect yourself with Hiranyagarbha or the cosmic Prana and imagine that the cosmic energy is flowing through your hands towards the patient. The patient will at once feel warmth, relief and strength. You can cure headache, intestinal colic or any other disease by massage and by your magnetic touch. When you massage the liver, spleen, stomach or any other portion or organ of the body you can speak to the cells and give them orders:"O cells! Discharge your functions properly. I command you to do so." They will obey your orders. They too have got subconscious intelligence. Repeat your Mantra when you pass your Prana to others. Try a few cases. You will gain competence. You can cure scorpion-sting also. Gently shampoo the leg and bring the poison down.

You can have extraordinary power of concentration, strong will and a perfectly healthy, strong body by Practising Pranayama regularly. You will have to direct the Prana consciously to unhealthy parts of the body. Suppose you have a sluggish liver. Sit on Padmasana. Close your eyes. Do Sukha Purvaka Pranayama. Direct the Prana to the region of the liver. Concentrate your mind there. Fix your attention to that area. Imagine that Prana is interpenetrating all the tissues and the cells of the lobes of the liver and doing its curative, regenerating and constructive work there. Faith, imagination, attention and interest play a very important part in curing diseases by taking Prana to the diseased areas.

During exhalation imagine that the morbid impurities of the liver are thrown out. Repeat this process 12 times in the morning and 12 times in the evening. Sluggishness of liver will vanish in a few days. This is a drugless treatment. This is nature-cure. You can take the Prana to any part of the body during the Pranayama and cure any kind of disease, be it acute or chronic. Try once or twice in healing yourself. Your convictions will grow stronger. Why do you cry like the lady who is crying for ghee when she has butter in her hand, when you have a cheap, potent, easily available remedy or agent 'Prana' at your command at all times! Use it judiciously. When you advance in your concentration and practice, you can cure many diseases by mere touch. In the advanced stages, many diseases are cured by mere will.

7. Distant Healing

This is known as "absent treatment" also. You can transmit Prana through space to your friend who is living at a distance. He should have a receptive mental attitude. You must feel yourself en rapport (in direct relation and in sympathy) with the people whom you heal with this Distant Healing method.

You can fix hours of appointment with them through correspondence. You can write to them: "Get ready at 8 p.m. Have a receptive mental attitude. Lie down in an easy-chair. Close your eyes. I shall transmit my Prana".

Say mentally to the patient, 'I am transmitting a supply of Prana (vital force)'. Do Kumbhaka when you send the Prana. Practise rhythmical breathing also. Have a mental image that the Prana is leaving your mind, passing through space, and is entering the system of the patient. The Prana travels unseen like the wireless (radio) waves and flashes like lightning across space. The Prana that is colored by the thought of the healer is projected outside. You can re-charge yourself with Prana by Practising Kumbhaka. This requires long, steady and regular practice.

Importance Of Pranayama

Tamas and Rajas constitute the covering or veil. This veil is removed by the practice of Pranayama. After the veil is removed, the real nature of the soul is realized. The Chitta is by itself made up of Sattvic particles, but it is enveloped by Rajas and Tamas, just as the fire is enveloped by smoke. There is no purificatory action greater than Pranayama. Pranayama gives purity, and the light of knowledge shines. The Karma of the Yogi, which covers up the discriminative knowledge, is annihilated by the practice of Pranayama. By the magic panorama of desire, the essence, which is luminous by nature, is covered up and the Jiva or individual soul is directed towards vice. This Karma of the Yogi which covers up the Light and binds him to repeated births, becomes attenuated by the practice of Pranayama every moment and is destroyed eventually.

Dharanasu cha Yogyata Manasah: "The mind becomes fit for concentration" Yoga Sutra (II-53). You will be able to concentrate the mind nicely after this veil of the light has been removed. The mind will be quite steady like the flame in a windless place as the disturbing energy has been removed. The word Pranayama is sometimes used collectively for inhalation, retention and exhalation of breath and sometimes for each of these severally. When the Prana Vayu moves in Akasa Tattva, the breathing will be lessened. At this time it will be easy to stop the breath. The velocity of the mind will be slowly lessened by the Pranayama. It will induce Vairagya also.

Benefits Of Pranayama

This body becomes lean, strong and healthy. Too much fat is reduced. There is lustre in the face. Eyes sparkle like diamonds. The practitioner becomes very handsome. Voice becomes sweet and melodious. The inner Anahata sounds are distinctly heard. The student is free from all sorts of diseases. He gets established in Brahmacharya. Semen gets firm and steady. The Jatharagni (gastric fire) is augmented.

The student becomes so perfected in Brahmacharya that his

mind will not be shaken even if a fairy tries to embrace him. Appetite becomes keen. Nadis are purified. Vikshepa is removed and the mind becomes one-pointed. Rajas and Tamas are destroyed. The mind is prepared for Dharana and Dhyana. The excretions become scanty. Steady practice arouses the inner spiritual force and brings in spiritual light, happiness and peace of mind. It makes him an Oordhvareto-Yogi. All psychic powers are obtained. Advanced students only will get all the benefits.

Instructions On Pranayama

1. Early morning, answer the calls of nature and sit for the Yogic practices. Practise Pranayama in a dry, welt-ventilated room. Pranayama requires deep concentration and attention. Do not keep anyone by your side.

2. Before you sit for Pranayama practice, thoroughly clean the nostrils. When you finish the practice, take a cup of milk or light tiffin after 10 minutes.

3. Strictly avoid too much talking, eating, sleeping, mixing with friends and exertion. Take a little ghee with rice when you take your meals. This will lubricate the bowels and allow Vayu to move downwards freely.

4. Some people twist the muscles of the face when they do Kumbhaka. It should be avoided. It is also a symptom to indicate that they are going beyond their capacity. This must be strictly avoided. Such people cannot have a regulated Rechaka and Puraka.
5. Pranayama can also be performed as soon as you get up from

bed and just before Japa and meditation. It will make your body light and you will enjoy the meditation. You must have a routine according to your convenience and time.

6. Do not shake the body unnecessarily. By shaking the body often the mind also is disturbed. Do not scratch the body every now and then. The Asana should be steady and as firm as a rock when you do Pranayama, Japa and meditation.

7. In all the exercises, repeat Rama, Siva, Gayatri, or any other Mantra, mere number or any other time-unit according to your inclination. Gayatri or OM is the best for Pranayama. In the beginning you must observe some time-unit for Puraka, Kumbhaka and Rechaka. The time-unit and the proper ratio comes by itself when you do the Puraka, Kumbhaka and Rechaka as long as you can do them comfortably. When you have advanced in the practice, you need not count or keep any unit. You will be naturally established in the normal ratio through force of habit.

8. For some days in the beginning you must count the number and see how you progress. In the advanced stages, you need not distract the mind in counting. The lungs will tell you when you have finished the required number.

9. Do not perform the Pranayama till you are fatigued. There must be always joy and exhilaration of spirit during and after the practice. You should come out of the practice fully invigorated and refreshed. Do not bind yourself by too many rules (Niyamas).

10. Do not take bath immediately after Pranayama is over. Take

rest for half an hour. If you get perspiration during the practice, do not wipe it with a towel. Rub it with your hand. Do not expose the body to the chill draughts of air when you perspire.

11. Always inhale and exhale very slowly. Do not make any sound. In Pranayamas like Bhastrika and Kapalabhati, you can produce a mild or the lowest possible sound.

12. You should not expect the benefits after doing it for 2 or 3 minutes only for a day or two. At least you must have 15 minutes' daily practice in the beginning regularly for days together. There will be no use if you jump from one exercise to another every day.

13. Patanjali does not lay much stress on the practice of different kinds of Pranayama. He mentions: "Exhale slowly, then inhale and retain the breath. You will get a steady and calm mind." It was only the Hatha Yogins who developed Pranayama as a science and who have mentioned various exercises to suit different persons.

14. A neophyte should do Puraka and Rechaka only without any Kumbhaka for some days. Take a long time to do Rechaka. The proportion for Puraka and Rechaka is 1:2.

15. "Pranayama in its popular and preparatory form may be practiced by everyone in any posture whatsoever, sitting or walking; and yet it is sure to show its benefits. For those who practise it in accordance with the prescribed methods, fructification will be rapid."

16. Gradually increase the period of Kumbhaka. Retain for 4 seconds in the first week, for 8 seconds in the second week and for 12 seconds in the third week and so on till you are able to retain the breath to your full capacity.

17. You must so nicely adjust the Puraka, Kumbhaka and Rechaka that you should not experience the feeling of suffocation or discomfort at any stage of Pranayama. You should never feel the necessity of catching hold of a few normal breaths between any two successive rounds. The duration of Puraka, Kumbhaka and Rechaka must be properly adjusted. Exercise due care and attention. Matters will turn out to be successful and easy.

18. You must not unnecessarily prolong the period of exhalation. If you prolong the time of Rechaka, the following inhalation will be done in a hurried manner and the rhythm will be disturbed. You must so carefully regulate the Puraka, Kumbhaka and Rechaka that you must be able to do with absolute comfort and care, not only of one Pranayama but also the full course or required rounds of Pranayama. I have to repeat this often. Experience and practice will make one perfect. Be steady. Another important factor is that you must have efficient control over the lungs at the end of Kumbhaka to enable you to do the Rechaka smoothly and in proportion with the Puraka.

HATHA YOGA PRADIPIKA ON MUDRAS

1. As the chief of the snakes is the support of the earth with all the mountains and forests on it, so all the Tantras (Yoga practices) rest on the Kundalini. (The Vertebral column.)

2. When the sleeping Kundalini awakens by favor of a guru, then all the lotuses (in the six chakras or centers) and all the knots are pierced through.

3. Susumna (Sunya Padavi) becomes a main road for the passage of Prana, and the mind then becomes free from all connections (with its objects of enjoyments) and Death is then evaded.

4. Susumna, Sunya, Padavi, Brahma Randhra, Maha Patha, Smâsana, Sambhavi, Madhya Marga, are names of one and the same thing.

5. In order, therefore, to awaken this goddess, who is sleeping at the entrance of Brahma Dwara (the great door), mudras should be practiced well.

The Mudras.

6. Maha Mudra, Maha Bandha, Maha Vedha, Khechari, Uddiyana Bandha, Mula Bandha, Jalandhara Bandha.

Viparita Karani, Vijroli, and Sakti Chalana. These are the ten Mudras which annihilate old age and death.

They have been explained by Adi Natha (Siva) and give eight kinds of divine wealth. They are loved by all the Siddhas and are hard to attain even by the Marutas.

Note.--The eight Aiswarikis are: Anima (becoming small, like an atom), Mahima (becoming great, like akas, by drawing in atoms of prakriti), Garima (light things, like cotton becoming very heavy like mountains).

Prapti (coming within easy reach of everything; as touching the moon with the little finger, while standing on the earth).

Prakamya (non-resistance to the desires, as entering the earth like water).

Isata (mastery over matter and objects made of it).

Vasitwa (controlling the animate and inanimate objects).

9. These Mudras should be kept secret by every means, as one keeps one's box of jewelry, and should, on no account be told to any one, just as husband and wife keep their dealings secret.

The Maha Mudra.

10. Pressing the Yoni (perineum) with the heel of the left foot, and stretching forth the right foot, its toes should be grasped by the thumb and first finger 11-12. By stopping the throat (by Jalandhara Bandha) the air is drawn in from outside and carried down. Just as a snake struck with a stick becomes straight like a stick, in the same way, sakti (susumna)

becomes straight at once. Then the Kundalini becoming as it were dead, and, leaving both the Ida and the Pingala, enters the susumna (the middle passage).

13. It should be expelled then, slowly only and not violently. For this very reason, the best of wise men call it the Maha Mudra. This Muha Mudra has been propounded by great masters.

14. Great evils and pains, like death, are destroyed by it, and for this reason wise men call it the Maha Mudra.

15. Having practiced with the left nostril, it should be practiced with the right one; and, when the number on both sides becomes equal, then the mudra should be discontinued.

16. There is nothing wholesome or injurious; for the practice of this mudra destroys the injurious effects of all the rasas (chemicals). Even the deadliest of poisons, if taken, acts like nectar.

17. Consumption, leprosy, prolapsus anii, colic, and the diseases due to indigestion,-- all these irregularities are removed by the practice of this Maha Mudra.

18. This Maha Mudra has been described as the giver of great success (Siddhi) to men. It should be kept secret by every effort, and not revealed to any and everyone.

The Maha Bandha.

22. Some are of opinion that the closing of throat is not necessary here, for keeping the tongue pressed against the roots of the

upper teeth makes a good bandha (stop).

23. This stops the upward motion of all the nadis. Verily this Muha Bandha is the giver of great Siddhis.

24. This Maha Bandha is the most skillful means for cutting away the snares of death. It brings about the conjunction of the Triveni (Ida, Pingala and Susumna) and carries the mind to Kedar (the space between the eyebrows, which is the seat of Siva).

25. As beauty and loveliness, do not avail a woman without a husband, so the Maha Mudra and the Maha-Bandha are useless without the Maha Vedha.

The Maha Vedha.

26. Sitting with Maha Bandha, the Yogi should fill the air and keep his mind collected. The movements of the Vayus (Prana and Apana) should be stopped by closing the throat.

27. Resting both the hands equally on the ground, he should raise himself a little and strike his buttocks against the ground gently. The air, leaving both the passages (Ida and Pingala), starts into the middle one.

28. The union of the Ida and Pingala is effected, in order to bring about immortality. When the air becomes as it were dead (by leaving its course through the Ida and the Pingala) (i.e., when it has been kept confined), then it should be expelled.

29. The practice of this Maha Veda, giver of great Siddhis,

destroys old age, grey hair, and shaking of the body, and therefore it is practiced by the best masters.

30. These three are the great secrets. They are the destroyers of old age and death, increase the appetite, confer the accomplishments of Anima, etc.

31. They should be practiced in 8 ways, daily and hourly. They increase collection of good actions and lesson the evil ones. People, instructed well, should begin their practice, little by little, first.

Kechari Mudra

32. The Kèchari Mudra is accomplished by thrusting the tongue into the gullet, by turning it over itself, and keeping the eyesight in the middle.

33. To accomplish this, the tongue is lengthened by cutting the fraenum linguae, moving, and pulling it. When it can touch the space between the eyebrows, then the Kechari can be accomplished.

34. Taking a sharp, smooth and clean instrument, of the shape of a cactus leaf, the frenulum of the tongue should be cut a little (as much as a hairs thickness), at a time.

35. Then rock salt and yellow myrobalan (both powdered) should be rubbed in. On the 7th day, it should again be cut a hair's breadth.

36. One should go on doing thus, regularly for six months. At the

end of six months, the freanum of the tongue will be completely cut.

37. Turning the tongue upwards, it is fixed on three ways (esophagus, windpipe and palate). Thus it makes the Khachari Mudra, and is called the Vyoma Chakra.

38. The Yogi who sits for a minute turning his tongue upwards, is saved from poisons, diseases, death, old age, etc.

39. He who knows the Kechari Mudra is not afflicted with disease, death, sloth, sleep, hunger, thirst, and swooning.

40. He who knows the Kechari Mudra, is not troubled by diseases, is not stained with karmas, and is not snared by time.

41. The Siddhas have devised this Kechari Mudra from the fact that the m ind and the tongue reach akasa by its practice.

42. If the hole behind the palate be stopped with Kechari by turning the tongue upwards, then bindu cannot leave its place even if a women were embraced.

43. If the Yogi drinks Somarasa (juice) by sitting with the tongue turned backwards and mind concentrated, there is no doubt he conquers death within 15 days.

44. If the Yogi, whose body is full of Somarasa, were bitten by Takshaka (snake), its poison cannot permeate his body.

45. As fire is inseparably connected with the wood and light is connected with the wick and oil, so does the soul not leave the body full of nectar exuding from the Soma.

(Note.--Soma (Chandra) is described later on located in the thousand-petalled lotus in the human brain, and is the same as is seen on Sivas' head in pictures, and from which a sort of juice exudes. It is the restraining of this exudation which makes one immortal.)

46. Those who eat the flesh of the cow and drink the immortal liquor daily, are regarded by me men of noble family. Others are but a disgrace to their families.

(Note. Translation: Fortunate are the parents and blessed is the country and the family where a Yogi is born. Anything given to such a Yogi, becomes immortal. One, who discriminates between Purusa and Prakriti, purges the sins of a million incarnations, by seeing, speaking, and touching such men (i.e. Yogi).

A Yogi far exceeds a thousand householders, a hundred vanapraasthas, and a thousand Brahmacharis.

Who can know the reality of the Raja Yoga? That country is very sacred where resides a man who knows it. By seeing and honoring him, generations of ignorant men get moksa, what to speak of those who are actually engaged in it. He knows internal and external yoga, deserves adoration from you and me, what if he is adored by the rest of mankind!

Those who engage in the great yoga, once or thrice daily, are to be known as masters of great wealth (mabeshwaras) or (Lords.)

47. The word (râsana[?]) means tongue; eating it is thrusting it in

the gullet which destroys great sins.

48. Immortal liquor is the nectar exuding from the moon (Chandra situated on the left side of the space between the eyebrows). It is produced by the fire which is generated by thrusting the tongue.

49. If the tongue can touch with its end the hole from which falls the rasa (juice) which is saltish, bitter, sour, milky and similar to ghee and honey, one can drive away disease, destroy old age, can evade an attack of arms, become immortal in eight ways and can attract fairies.

50. He who drinks the clear stream of liquor of the moon (soma) falling from the brain to the sixteen-petalled lotus (in the heart), obtained by means of Prana by applying the tongue to the hole of the pendant in the palate, and by meditating on the great power (Kundalini), becomes free from disease and tender in body, like the stalk of a lotus, and the Yogi lives a very long life.51. On the top of the Meru (vertabral column), concealed in a hole, is the Somarasa (nectar of Chandra); the wise, whose intellect is not over-powered by Raja and Tamas gunas, but in whom Satwa guna is predominant, say there is the (universal spirit) atma in it. It is the source of the down-going Ida, Pingala and Susumna Nadis, which are the Ganges, the Yamuna and the Sarasvati. From that Chandra is shed the essence of the body which causes death of men. It should, therefore, be stopped from shedding. This (Khechari Mudra) is a very good instrument for this purpose. There is no other means of achieving this end.

52. This hole is the generator of knowledge and is the source of the five streams (Ida, Pingala, &c.). In that colorless vacuum, Khechari Mudra should be established.

53. There is only one seed germinating the whole universe from it; and there is only one Mudra, called Khachari. There is only one deva (god) without any one's support, and there is one condition called Manonmani.

The Uddiyana Bandha.

54. Uddiyana is so called by the Yogis, because by its practice the Prana (vayu), flies (flows) in the Susumna.

55. Uddiyana is so called, because the great bird, Prana, tied to it, flies without being fatigued. It is explained below.

56. The belly above the navel is pressed backwards towards the spine. This Uddiyana Bandha is like a lion for the elephant of death.

57. Uddiyana is always very easy, when learnt from a guru. The practiser of this, if old, becomes young again.

58. The portions above and below the navel, should be drawn backwards towards the spine. By practicing this for six months one can undoubtedly conquer death.

59. Of all the Bandhas, Uddiyana is the best; for by binding it firmly liberation comes spontaneously.

The Mula Bandha.

60. Pressing Yoni (perineum) with the heel, contract up the anus. By drawing the Apana thus, Mula Bandha is made.

61. The Apana, naturally inclining downward, is made to go up by force. This Mula Bandha is spoken of by Yogis as done by contracting the anus.

62. Pressing the heel well against the anus, draw up the air by force, again and again till it (air) goes up.

63. Prana, Apana, Nada and Bindu uniting into one in this way, give success in Yoga, undoubtedly.

64. By the purification of Prana, and Apana, urine and excrements decrease. Even an old man becomes young by constantly practicing Mula Bandha.

65. Going up the Apana enters the zone of fire, i.e., the stomach. The flame of fire struck by the air is thereby lengthened.

(Note. In the center of the body is the seat of fire, like heated gold. In men it is triangular, in quadrupeds square, in birds circular. There is a long thin flame in this fire. It is gastric fire.)

66. These, fire and Apana, go to the naturally hot Prana, which, becoming inflamed thereby, causcs burning sensation in the body.

67. The Kundalini, which has been sleeping all this time, becomes well heated by this means and awakens well. It becomes straight like a serpent, struck dead with a stick.

68. It enters the Brahma Nadi, just like a serpent enters its hole.

Therefore, the Yogi should always practice this Mula Bandha.

The Jalandhara Bandha.

69. Contract the throat and press the chin firmly against the chest. This is called Jalandhara Bandha, which destroys old age and death.

70. It stops the opening (hole) of the group of Nadis, through which the juice from the sky (from the Soma or Chandra in the brain) falls down. It is, therefore, called the Jalandhara Bandha -- the destroyer of a host of diseases of thhhhe throat.

71. In Jalandhara Bandha, the indications of a perfect contraction of throat are, that the nectar does not fall into the fire (the Surya situated in the navel), and the air is not disturbed.

72. The two Nadis should be stopped firmly by contracting the throat. This is called the middle circuit or center (Madhya Chakra), and it stops the 16 adharas (i.e., vital parts).

(Note-The sixteen vital parts mentioned by renowned Yogis are the (1) thumbs, (2) ankles, (3) knees, (5) the prepuce, (6) organs of generation, (7) the navel, (8) the heart, (9) the neck, (10) the throat, (11) the palate, (12) the nose, (13) the middle of the eyebrows, (14) the forehead, (15) the head and (16) the Brahmarandra.)

73. By drawing up the mulasthana (anus), Uddiyana Bandha should be performed. The flow of the air should be directed to the Susumna, by closing the Ida and the Pingala.

74. The Prana becomes calm and latent by this means, and thus there is no death, old age, disease, etc.

75. These three Bandhas are the best of all and have been practiced by the masters. Of all the means of success in Hatha Yoga, they are known to the Yogis as the chief ones.

76. The whole of the nectar, possessing divine qualities, which exudes from the Soma (Chandra) is devoured by the Surya; and, owing to this, the body becomes old.

77. To remedy this, the opening of the Surya is avoided by excellent means. It is to be learnt best by instructions from a guru; but not by even a million discussions.

The Viparita Karani.

78. Above the navel and below the palate respectively, are the Surya and the Chandra. The exercise, called the Viparita Karani, is learnt from the guru's instructions.

79. This exercise increases the appetite; and, therefore, one who practices it, should obtain a good supply of food. If the food be scanty, it will burn him at once.

80. Place the head on the ground and the feet up into the sky, for a second only the first day, and increase this time daily.

81. After six months, the wrinkles and gray hair are not seen. He who practices it daily, even for two hours, conquers death.

The Vajroli.

82. Even if one who lives a wayward life, without observing any rules of Yoga, but performs Vajroli, deserves success and is a Yogi.

83. Two things are necessary for this, and these are difficult to get for the ordinary people -- (1) milk and (2) a woman behaving, as desired.

84. By practicing to draw in the bindu, discharged during cohabitation, whether one be a man or a woman, one obtains success in the practice of Vajroli.

85. By means of a pipe, one should blow air slowly into the passage in the male organ. [Urethra.]

86. By practice, the discharged bindu is drawn out. One can draw back and preserve one's own discharged bindu.

87. The Yogi who can protect his bindu thus, overcomes death; because death comes by discharging bindu, and life is prolonged by its preservation.

88. By preserving bindu, the body of the Yogi emits a pleasing smell. There is no fear of death, so long as the bindu is well-established in the body.

89. The bindu of men is under control of the mind, and life is dependant on the bindu. Hence, mind and bindu should be protected by all means.

The Sahajoli.

90. Sahajoli and Amaroli are only the different kinds of Vajroli. Ashes from burnt up cow dung should be mixed with water.

91. Being free from the exercise of Vajroli, man and woman should both rub it on their bodies.

92. This is called Sahajoli, and should be relied on by Yogis. It does good and gives moksa.

93. This Yoga is achieved by courageous wise men, who are free from sloth, and cannot be accomplished by the slothful.

The Amaroli.

94. In the doctrine of the sect of the Kapalikas, the Amaroli is the drinking of the mid stream; leaving the 1st, as it is a mixture of too much bile and the last, which is useless.

95. He who drinks Amari, snuff it daily, and practices Vajroli, is called practicing Amaroli.

96. The bindu discharged in the practice of Vajroli should be mixed with ashes, and the rubbing it on the best parts of the body gives divine sight.

The Sakti chalana.

97. Kutilanga (crooked-bodied), Kundalini, Bhujangi (a she-serpent) Sakti, Ishwari, Kuundali, Arunddhati, -- all these words are synonymous.

98. As a door is opened with a key, so the Yogi opens the door of mukti by opening Kundalini by means of Hatha Yoga.

99. The Parameswari (Kundalini) sleeps, covering the hole of the passage by which one can go to the seat of Brahma which is free from pains.100. Kundali Sakti sleeps on the bulb, for the purpose of giving moksa to Yogis and bondage to the ignorant. He who knows it, knows Yoga.

101. Kundali is of a bent shape, and has been described to be like a serpent. He who has moved that Sakti is no doubt Mukta (released from bondage).

102. Youngster Tapaswini (a she-ascetic), laying between the Ganges and the Yamuni, (Ida and Pingala) should be caught hold of by force, to get the highest position.

103. Ida is called the goddess Ganges, Pingala goddess Yamuna. In the middle of the Ida and the Pingala is the infant widow, Kundali.

104. This sleeping she-serpent should be awakened by catching hold of her tail. By the force of Hatha, the Sakti leaves her sleep, and starts upwards.

105. This she-serpent is situated in Muladhar. She should be caught and moved daily, morning and evening, for 1/2 a prahar (1 1/2 hours), by filling with air through Pingala by the Paridhana method. 106. The bulb is above the anus, a vitasti (12 angulas) long, and measures 4 angulas (3 inches) in extent and is soft and white, and appears as if a folded

cloth.

107. Keeping the feet in Vajra-âsana (Padma-âsana), hold them firmly with the hands. The position of the bulb then will be near the ankle joint, where it should be pressed.

108. The Yogi, sitting with Vajra-âsana and having moved Kundali, should perform Bhastrika to awaken the Kundali soon.

109. Bhanu (Surya, near the navel) should be contracted (by contracting the navel) which will move the Kundali. There is no fear for him who does so, even if he has entered the mouth of death.

110. By moving this, for two muhurtas, it is drawn up a little by entering the Susumna (spinal column).

111. By this Kundalini leaves the entrance of the Susumna at once, and the Prana enters it of itself.

112. Therefore, this comfortably sleeping Arundhati should always be moved; for by so doing the Yogi gets rid of diseases.

113. The Yogi, who has been able to move the Sakti deserves success. It is useless to say more, suffice it to say that he conquers death playfully.

114. The Yogi observing Brahmacharya (continence) and always eating sparingly gets success within 40 days by practice with Kundali.

115. After moving the Kundali, plenty of Bhastra should be performed. By such practice, he has no fear from the god of death.

116. There is no other way, but the practice of the Kundali, for washing away the impurities of 72,000 Nadis.

117. This middle Nadi becomes straight by steady practice of postures; Pranayama and Mudras of Yogis.

118. Those whose sleep has decreased by practice and mind has become calm by samadhi, get beneficial accomplishments by Sambhavi and other Mudras.

119. Without Raja Yoga, this earth, the night, and the Mudras, be they howsoever wonderful, do not appear beautiful.

(Note.--Raja Yoga=âsana. Earth=steadiness, calmness. Night=Kumbhaka; cessations of the activity of the Prana, just as King's officials cease moving at night. Hence night means absence of motion, i.e., Kumbhaka.)

120. All the practices relating to air should be performed with concentrated mind. A wise man should not allow his mind to wander away.

121. These are the Mudras, as explained by Adinatha (Siva). Every one of them is the giver of great accomplishments to the practiser.

122. He is really the guru and not to be considered as Isvara in human form who teaches the Mudras as handed down from

guru to guru.

123. Engaging in practice, by putting faith in his words, one gets the Siddhis of Anima, etc., as also evades death.

End of The Exposition of the Mudras.

HATHA YOGA PRADIPIKA ON PRANAYAMA

1. Posture becoming established, a Yogi, master of himself, eating salutary and moderate food, should practice pranayama, as instructed by his guru.

2. Respiration being disturbed, the mind becomes disturbed. By restraining respiration, the Yogi gets steadiness of mind.

3. So long as the (breathing) air stays in the body, it is called life. Death consists in the passing out of the (breathing) air. It is, therefore, necessary to restrain the breath.

4. The breath does not pass through the middle channel (Susumna), owing to the impurities of the nadis. How can then success be attained, and how can there be the unmani avastha.

5. When the whole system of the nadis which is full of impurities, is cleaned, then the Yogi becomes able to control the Prana.

6. Therefore, Pranayama should be performed daily with satwika buddhi (intellect free from raja and tama or activity and sloth), in order to drive out the impurities of the Susumna.

Methods of performing Pranayama.

7. Sitting in the Padmâsana posture the Yogi should fill in the air through the left nostril (closing the right one); and,

keeping it confined according to one's ability, it should be expelled slowly through the Surya (right nostril).

8. Then, drawing in the air through the Surya slowly, the belly should be filled, and after performing Kumbhaka as before, it should be expelled slowly through the Chandra (left nostril).

9. Inhaling thus through the one, through which it was expelled, and having restrained it there, till possible, it should be exhaled through the other, slowly and not forcibly.

10. If the air be inhaled through the left nostril, it should be expelled again through the other, and filling it through the right nostril, confining it there, it should be expelled through the left nostril. By practicing in this way, through the right and the left nostrils alternately, the whole of the collection of the nadis of the yamis (practisers) becomes clean, i.e., free from impurities, after 3 months and over.

11. Kumbhakas should be performed gradually four times during day and night (i.e., morning, noon, evening and midnight), till the number of Kumbhakas for one time is 80 and for day and night together it is 320.

12. In the beginning there is perspiration, in the middle stage there is quivering, and in the last or third stage, one obtains steadiness; and then the breath should be made steady or motionless.

13. The perspiration exuding from exertion of practice should be

rubbed into the body (and not wiped), as by so doing the body becomes strong.

14. During the first stage of practice the food consisting of milk and ghee is wholesome. When the practice becomes established, no such restriction is necessary.

15. Just as lions, elephants and tigers are controlled by and by, so the breath is controlled by slow degrees, otherwise (i.e., by being hasty or using too much force) it kills the practitioner himself.

16. When Pranayama, etc., are performed properly, they eradicate all diseases; but an improper practice generates diseases.

17. Hiccough, asthma, cough, pain in the head, the ears, and the eyes; these and other various kinds of diseases are generated by the disturbance of the breath.

18. The air should be expelled with proper tact and should be filled in skillfully; and when it has been kept confined properly it brings success.

N.B.--The above caution is necessary to warn the aspirants against omitting any instruction; and in their zeal to gain success or siddhis early, to begin the practice, either by using too much force in filling in, confining and expelling the air, or by omitting any instructions, it may cause unnecessary pressure on their ears, eyes, &c., and cause pain.

Every word in the instructions is full of meaning and is

necessarily used in the slokas, and should be followed very carefully and with due attention. Thus there will be nothing to fear whatsoever. We are inhaling and exhaling the air throughout our lives without any sort of danger, and Pranayama being only a regular form of it, there should be no cause to fear.)

19. When the nadis become free from impurities, and there appear the outward signs of success, such as lean body and glowing color, then one should feel certain of success.

20. By removing the impurities, the air can be restrained, according to one's wish and the appetite is increased, the divine sound is awakened, and the body becomes healthy.

21. If there be excess of fat or phlegm in the body, the six kinds of kriyas (duties) should be performed first. But others, not suffering from the excess of these, should not perform them.

22. The six kinds of duties are: Dhauti, Basti, Neti, Trataka, Nauti and Kapala Bhati. These are called the six actions.

23. These six kinds of actions which cleanse the body should be kept secret. They produce extraordinary attributes and are performed with earnestness by the best Yogis.

The Dhauti.

24. A strip of cloth, about 3 inches wide and 15 cubits long, is pushed in (swallowed), when moist with warm water, through the passage shown by the guru, and is taken out again. This is called Dhauti Karma.

N.B.-- The strip should be moistened with a little warm water, and the end should be held with the teeth. It is swallowed slowly, little by little: thus, first day 1 cubit, 2nd day 2 cubits, 3rd day 3 cubits, and so on. After swallowing it the stomach should be given a good, round motion from left to right, and then it should be taken out slowly and gently.)

25. There is no doubt, that cough, asthma, enlargement of the spleen, leprosy, and 20 kinds of diseases born of phlegm, disappear by the practice of Dhauti Karma.

The Basti.

26. Squatting in navel deep water, and introducing a six inches long, smooth piece of 1/2 an inch diameter pipe, open at both ends, half inside the anus; it (anus) should be drawn up (contracted) and then expelled. This washing is called Basti Karma.

27. By practicing this Basti Karma, colic, enlarged spleen, and dropsy, arising from the disorders of Vata (air), pitta (bile) and kapha (phlegm), are all cured.

28. By practicing Basti with water, the Dhatus, the Indriyas and the mind become calm. It gives glow and tone to the body and increases the appetite. All the disorders disappear.

The Neti.

29. A cord made of threads and about six inches long, should be passed through the passage of the nose and the end taken out in the mouth. This is called by adepts the Neti Karma.

30. The Neti is the cleaner of the brain and giver of divine sight. It soon destroys all the diseases of the cervical and scapular regions.

The Tratika.

31. Being calm, one should gaze steadily at a small mark, till eyes are filled with tears. This is called Tratika by acharyas.

32. Tratika destroys the eye diseases and removes sloth, etc. It should be kept secret very carefully, like a box of jewelry.

The Nauli.

33. Sitting on the toes with heels raised above the ground, and the palms resting on the ground, and in this bent posture the belly is moved forcibly from left to right, just as in vomiting. This is called by adepts the Nauli Karma.

34. It removes dyspepsia, increases appetite and digestion, and is like the goddess of creation, and causes all happiness. It dries up all the disorders. This is an excellent exercise in Hatha Yoga.

The Kapala Bhati.

35. When inhalation and exhalation are performed very quickly, like a pair of bellows of a blacksmith, it dries up all the disorders from the excess of phlegm, and is known as Kapala Bhati.

36. When Pranayama is performed after getting rid of obesity born of the defects of phlegm, by the performance of the six

duties, it easily brings success.

37. Some acharyas (teachers) do not advocate any other practice, being of opinion that all the impurities are dried up by the practice of Pranayama.

Gija Karani.

38. By carrying the Apana Vayu up to the throat, the food, etc., in the stomach are vomited, By degrees, the system of Nadis (Sankhini) becomes known. This is called in Hatha as Gaja Karani.

39. Brahna and other Devas were always engaged in the exercise of Pranayama, and, by means of it, got rid of the fear of death. Therefore, one should practice pranayama regularly.

40. So long as the breath is restrained in the body, so long as the mind is undisturbed, and so long as the gaze is fixed between the eyebrows, there is no fear from Death.

41. When the system of Nadis becomes clear of the impurities by properly controlling the prana, then the air, piercing the entrance of the Susumna, enters it easily.

Manomani.

42. Steadiness of mind comes when the air moves freely in the middle. That is the manonmani condition, which is attained when the mind becomes calm.

43. To accomplish it, various Kumbhakas are performed by those who are expert in the methods; for, by the practice of

different Kumbhakas, wonderful success is attained.

Different kinds of Kumbhakas.

44. Kumbhakas are of eight kinds, viz., Surya Bhedan, Ujjayi, Sitkari, Sitali, Bhastrika, Bhramari, Murchha, and Plavini.

45. At the end of Puraka, Jalandhara Bandha should be performed, and at the end of Kumbhaka, and at the beginning of Rechaka, Uddiyana Bandhas should not be performed.

(N.B.--Puraka is filling in of the air from the outside.)

46. Kumbhaka is the keeping the air confined inside. Rechaka is expelling the confined air. The instructions for Puraka, Kumbhaka and Rechaka will be found at the proper place and it should be carefully followed. By drawing up from below (Mula Bandha) and contracting the throat (Jalanddhara Bandha) and by pulling back the middle of the front portion of the body (i.e., belly), the Prana goes to the Brahma Nadi (Susumna).

(N.B.-- The middle hole, through the vertebral column, through which the spinal cord passes, is called the Susumna Nadi of the Yogis. The two other sympathetic cords, one on each side of the spinal cord, are called the Ida and the Pingala Nadis. These will be described later on.)

47. By pulling up the Apana Vayu and by forcing the Prana Vayu down the throat, the yogi, liberated from old age, becomes young, as it were 16 years old.
(Note.--The seat of the Prana is the heart; of the Apana anus;

of the Samana the region about the navel; of Udana the throat; while the Vyana moves throughout the body.)

Surya Bhedana.

48. Taking any comfortable posture and performing the âsana, the Yogi should draw in air slowly, through the right nostril.

49. Then it should be confined within, so that it fills from the nails to the tips of the hair, and let it out through the left nostril slowly.

(Note.-- This is to be done alternately with both the nostrils, drawing in through one, expelling through the other, and vice versa.)

50. This excellent Surya Bhedana cleanses the forehead (frontal sinuses), destroys the disorders of Vata, and removes the worms, and, therefore, it should be performed again and again.

(Note – Translation) :

1. I am going to describe the procedure of the practice of Yoga, in order that Yogis may succeed. A wise man should leave his bed in the Usa Kala (i.e., at the peep of dawn or 4 o'clock) in the morning.

2. Remembering his guru over his head, and his desired deity in his heart, after answering the calls of nature, and cleaning his mouth, he should apply Bhasma (ashes).

3. In a clean spot, clean room and charming ground, he should

spread a soft âsana (cloth for sitting on). Having seated on it and remembering in his mind his guru and his god.

4. Having extolled the place and the time and taking up the vow thus: 'To day by the grace of God, I will perform Pranayamas with âsanas for gaining Samadhi (trance) and its fruits.'

He should salute the infinite Deva, Lord of the Nagas, to insure success in the âsanas (postures).

5. Salutation to the Lord of the Nagas, who is adorned with thousands of heads, set with brilliant jewels (manis), and who has sustained the whole universe, nourishes it, and is infinite. After this he should begin his exercise of âsanas and when fatigued, he should practice sava âsana. Should there be no fatigue, he should not practice it.

6. Before Kumbhaka, he should perform Viparita Karni Mudra, in order that he may be able to perform Jalandhar bandha comfortably.

7. Sipping a little water, he should begin the exercise of Pranayama, after saluting Yogindras, as described in the Kurma Purana, in the words of Siva.

8. Such as "Saluting Yogindras and their disciples and guru Vinayaka, the Yogi should unite with me with composed mind."

9. While practicing, he should sit with Siddhâsana, and having performed bandha and Kumbhaka, should begin with 10 Pranayamas the first day, and go on increasing 6 daily.

10. With composed mind 80 Kumbhakas should be performed at a time; beginning first with the chandra (the left nostril) and then the surya (the right nostril).

11. This has been spoken of by wise men as Anuloma and Viloma. Having practiced Surya Bhedan, with Bandhas, the wise man should practice Ujjayi and then Sitkari Sitali, and Bhastrika, he may practice others or not.

12. He should practice mudras properly, as instructed by his guru. Then sitting with Padmâsana, he should hear anahata nada attentively.

13. He should resign the fruits of all his practice reverently to God, and, on rising on completion of the practice, a warm bath should be taken.

14. The bath should bring all the daily duties briefly to an end. At noon also a little rest should be taken at the end of the exercise, and then food should be taken.

15. Yogis should always take wholesome food and never anything unwholesome. After dinner he should eat Ilachi or lavanga.

16. Some like camphor, and betel leaf. To the Yogis, practicing Pranayama, betel leaf without powders, i.e., lime, nuts and katha, is beneficial.

17. After taking food he should read books treating of salvation, or hear Puranas and repeat the name of God.

18. In the evening the exercise should begin after finishing Sandyha, as before, beginning the practice 3 ghatika or one hour before the sunsets.

19. Evening sandhya should always be performed after practice, and Hatha Yoga should be practiced at midnight.

20. Viparita Karni is good to be practiced in the evening and at midnight, and not just after eating, as it does no good at this time.)

Ujjayi.

51. Having closed the opening of the Nadi (larynx), the air should be drawn in such a way that it goes touching from the throat to the chest, and making noise while passing.

52. It should be restrained, as before, and then let out through the Ida (the left nostril). This removes slesma (phlegm) in the throat and increases the appetite.

53. It destroys the defects of the nadis, dropsy and disorders of Dhatu (humors). Ujjayi should be performed in all conditions of life, even while walking or sitting.

Sitkari.

54. Sitkari is performed by drawing in the air through the mouth, keeping the tongue between the lips. The air thus drawn in should not be expelled through the mouth. By practicing in this way, one becomes next to the God of love and beauty.

55. He is regarded adorable by the Yoginis and becomes the

destroyer of the cycle of creation. He is not afflicted with hunger, thirst, sleep or lassitude.

56. The Satwa of his body becomes free from all disturbances. In truth, he becomes the lord of the Yogis in this world.

Sitali.

57. As in the above (Sitkari), the tongue to be protruded a little out of the lips, when the air is drawn in. It is kept confined, as before, and then expelled slowly through the nostrils.

58. This Sitali Kumbhaka cures colic, (enlarged) spleen, fever, disorders of bile, hunger, thirst, and counteracts poisons.

The Bhastrika.

59. The Padma âsana consists in crossing the feet and placing them on both the thighs; it is the destroyer of all sins.

60. Binding the Padma-âsana and keeping the body straight, closing the mouth carefully, let the air be expelled through the nose.

61. It should be filled up to the lotus of the heart, by drawing it in with force, making noise and touching the throat, the chest and the head.

62. It should be expelled again and filled again and again as before, just as a pair of bellows of the blacksmith is worked.

63. In the same way, the air of the body should be moved intelligently, filling it through Suyra when fatigue is

experienced.

64. The air should be drawn in through the right nostril by pressing the thumb against the left side of the nose, so as to close the left nostril; and when filled to the full, it should be closed with the fourth finger (the one next to the little finger) and kept confined.

65. Having confined it properly, it should be expelled through the Ida (left nostril). This destroys Vata, pitta (bile) and phlegm and increases the digestive power (the gastric fire).

66. It quickly awakens the Kundalini, purifies the system, gives pleasure, and is beneficial. It destroys phlegm and the impurities accumulated at the entrance of the Brahma Nadi.

67. This Bhastrika should be performed plentifully, for it breaks the three knots: Brahma granthi (in the chest), Visnu granthi (in the throat), and Rudra granthi (between the eyebrows) of the body.

The Bhramari.

68. By filling the air with force, making noise like Bhringi (wasp), and expelling it slowly, making noise in the same way; this practice causes a sort of ecstasy in the minds of Yogindras.

The Murchha.

69. Closing the passages with Jalandhar Bandha firmly at the end of Puraka, and expelling the air slowly, is called

Murchha, from its causing the mind to swoon and give comfort.

The Plavini.

70. When the belly is filled with air and the inside of the body is filled to its utmost with air, the body floats on the deepest water, like a leaf of a lotus.

71. Considering Puraka (Filling), Rechaka (expelling) and Kumhaka (confining), Pranayama is of three kinds, but considering it accompanied by Puraka and Rechaka, and without these, it is of two kinds only, i.e., Sabita (with) and Kevala (alone).

72. Exercise in Sahita should be continued till success in Kevala is gained. This latter is simply confining the air with ease, without Rechaka and Puraka.

73. In the practice of Kevala Pranayama when it can be performed successfully without Rechaka and Puraka, then it is called Kevala Kumbhaka.

74. There is nothing in the three worlds which may be difficult to obtain for him who is able to keep the air confined according to pleasure, by means of Kevala Kumbhaka.

75. He obtains the position of Raja Yoga undoubtedly. Kundalini awakens by Kumbhaka, and by its awakening, Susumna becomes free from impurities.

76. No success in Raja Yoga without Hatha Yoga, and no success

in Hatha Yoga without Raja Yoga. One should, therefore, practice both of these well, till complete success is gained.

77. On the completion of Kumbhaka, the mind should be given rest. By practicing in this way one is raised to the position of (succeeds in getting) Raja Yoga.

Indications of success in the practice of Hatha Yoga.

78. When the body becomes lean, the face glows with delight, Anahata-nada manifests, and eyes are clear, the body is healthy, bindu under control, and appetite increases, then one should know that the Nadis are purified and success in Hatha Yoga is approaching.

Manushya is 82 years old. Looking at the life he has led, his eyes are fixed on the group of students who have come to see him. "Guruji (renowned by the name of 'Guruji' 'Master') looks like 35 years of age" they look in awe at Manushya.

On the other hand, Manushya is thinking of the "Sacred Journey" as explained by Swami Rama of the Himalayas.

Swami Rama, brought up in the ancient cave monasteries, was not only a rare yogi but also a scientist and a social reformer. He was the author of numerous books, a poet, painter, master architect, musician, and an expert in many sciences and systems of philosophy. He founded the Himalayan International Institute of Yoga Science and Philosophy and the Himalayan Institute Hospital Trust and Medical College.

At the moment of death the following things take place. If the person is impious and quite sinful, the messengers of Yamaraja, called the Yamadutas, fierce, horrible looking persons with twisted features, copper red flaming hairs that stand on end, black in complexion and frightening to behold, appear at the deathbed of the person in question and drag him forcibly from his body with ropes and chains. This scene so frightens the person that he literally dies of fright. They then pack up the subtle body of the person in a bag, where they take the soul, now covered only by the subtle body of mind, intelligence and false ego, to the abode of Yamaraja for judgement. He is taken over long stretches of hot, dry sands, and along the way he is insulted in various ways by other horrible creatures and bitten by dogs. He is suffering terribly on this journey and he wishes it would end.

However, when it does end he is taken before Yamaraja, the fierce demigod in charge of death and punishing the sinful. He is forced to accept a position of suffering according to his sins in one of the hells which exists at the bottom of the universe, just above the Garbhodaka Ocean. In this hellish region called the Naraka, there are approximately 27 hellish places.

As an example of this a person who has engaged in the slaughter and eating of other innocent animals will enter into Krimibhojana, wherein he will exist as a worm who is eating the tail of another worm as that worm is eating his tail. There are many such hells just according to the crimes committed.

After such intense and horrible forms of suffering the living being is thrown again into the lower species of life just suited according to his sinful desires in his human life.

However, most persons are not quite that sinful and therefore they may expect a more normal departure from the body. At the time of death, death is denoted as the moment when the spirit soul departs from the material gross body. At that time the soul, covered by the subtle body of mind, intelligence and false ego, leaves the body. The subtle body always travels with the soul wherever he goes within this material world and therefore the living entity has a continuity of material experience throughout his different lifetimes.

Death may come from a variety of causes, but when it actually happens the first thing that a person experiences is total blackness. All is dark, but this lasts only for a moment. The Supersoul, situated right next to the soul, illuminates a hole which appears to the soul to be a light at the end of a tunnel. In fact the darkness which appears is the body but now that it is dead it is devoid of consciousness and now we are seeing it from the inside for the first time.

There are some 118 different passageways through which one might depart from the body. One may only go through one of these at the time of death. These passageways are called nadis, or channels of consciousness.

According to Garuda Purana 1.67 death occurs when both main (spine) nadis, Ida and Pingala, are at work. Under normal conditions they switch. One might understand them to be the major nerve channels of channels of energy flow within the body, but the exact medical synonym is not available to us at this time.

In any case one will depart from one of these nadis to his next destination. We do know that one who departs from the anus or genital goes to the lower regions, wherein one who departs from the upper portion of the body goes to the higher regions. Those who depart from the top of their skulls, from the hole known as the brahma randhra, the place where the three bones in the skull meet, will attain the regions of Brahman.

The Supersoul illuminates only one of these passageways according to the karma of the soul. He selects the passageway just according to the previous activities of the living entity and as soon as it is illuminated the soul naturally wants to move towards the light. As soon as he is out of the body, he feels relieved of the burden of the material frame and starts to move, naturally drawn towards his next form. At that time he will experience the world from the point of view of the subtle body and will see things much clearer than they are seen through the present body. Just try to imagine how much more beautiful the world must be when seen through spiritual eyes!

He then enters into the womb of a new mother as it is being impregnated by the father and awaits the time until the new body develops itself sufficiently to maintain consciousness. When the embryo is about seven months of age it is sufficiently developed to support consciousness and the baby awakens in his new body and immediately moves, sometimes kicking the mother from within in a vain attempt to get out of the horrible entanglement that he has found himself in.

If he is pious, this horrible condition of having the arms and legs jammed into the chest as one is bent over in the foetal position, causes the soul to pray to the Lord as follows, "O Lord, this condition is terrible.

Please save me from this situation and get me out of this womb immediately and I promise to serve You in this lifetime for sure." However, as soon as he takes his birth he becomes too much attached to all the attention and service being rendered him by mother and family members and he forgets all about serving the Lord and falls totally into maya again.

Avoid the process of rebirth, it is not auspicious in any way. The students have asked a question and Manushya, now, a Sage himself, is pondering on the question:

The question "Death has come to take me, how do I return it?" A crucial question, thinks Manushya, calmly, with twinkling eyes, Manushya replies:

"As long as the mind is undisturbed, and so long as the gaze is fixed between the eyebrows, there is no fear from Death"

At 149 years of age, Manushya still lives and looks like 45 years of age.

Adios my friends wish you live like Manushya and gain knowledge, like he did. Knowledge gained is fruitful only when it is adopted in our daily life.

Love & Light

Dr. Mohan Ph.D. (A.M.) / Dr. Geeta (Naturopathy)

LISTEN CAREFULLY, READ CAREFULLY, FOLLOW EACH WORD, THEN PRACTICE.

Day one of your life .. you are conceived ... how? Was the doctor in a hurry, was your mother relaxed? Were there any difficulties in your birth? Was it a forceps OR caesarian delivery?

All these questions are important to answer, as they can cause a turmoil with your life. But, how will you know this, Rebirthing? Let's see.

Memories of birth and your first breath

In order to be able to access your birth and conception issues, it is virtually necessary to access the information stored in your body concerning the first breath you ever took.

Now, this information is held in your body by the "freezing" or what is called the misalignment, subluxation of the spinal vertebrae known as T1, T2 and T2.

T1 is the big bump at the top of the spine and the base of the neck. T2 is the vertebrae below it. T3 particularly manifests in later life as what is known as the "Dowager's Hump".

Physiologically

Your main cardio-pulmonary nerve exits the spinal column between T1, T2 and T3 .. so any trauma stored in these vertebrae is going to affect the nerve responses to and from both the heart and the lungs.

This nerve also governs the functioning of the Thymus, Larynx, Trachea and Bronchi, thus affecting your breathing, your verbal expression, your swallowing and the mucous that builds up in the throat.

Source of the Damage

There is a very high probability of trauma being stored in T1 and T2 from being held upside down and belted on the bottom to make you breathe.

If you had to be pulled out of your mother's womb in any manner because she "froze", then any twisting of the neck by pulling on the head if you were in any way stuck in the shoulders will traumatize T1, T2 and T3. The use of forceps etc (and some of the other prehistoric instruments of fetal torture) will store this trauma both here and in the neck.

Your Process

If there is trauma stored here concerning your birth or your first breath, then you may not be able to access the birth/conception memories until/unless the memories of this trauma are released.

However, subsequent occasions where you "stop" your breath will build up onto the first breath memory and may need to be worked with first. This sort of thing can occur from "going unconscious" for any reason.

It is physically impossible to get out of your mind and into your body or to access your heart intelligence if this blockage exists in the base of your neck.

As the memories stored here are from very early in your life, there will be no words or language to describe the process or the experience.

Other symptoms.

The lower reflex point is the centre of the sacrum, S3, where the relationship with the world is stored. The nerves coming from here will affect both your sexuality and the way you digest food - either metaphorically or physically.

This point also governs the whole body elimination function - so, if you are holding on to your shit, metaphorically, then it may well be because you have trauma stored in T1, T2 and T3.

The upper reflex point is the base of the skull - where the skull joins the neck at the Atlas, good headaches, runny nose, eye problems.

Summary

So, you can see that a good pull when you were born can set you on the path to a whole lot of physical problems and disease which exacerbates with age.

The Release. *(Warning)* :

? This release can result in a lot of distress as symptoms come up from the body - along with all of the emotions repressed in the areas above mentioned.

? It can be beneficial to go to a chiropractor, osteopath, get a massage to shift or loosen the area, BUT, there will be no permanent release unless all of the other areas are considered and worked with as well.

? It is not something that you can do once - and think it's fixed.

What you can do for yourself.

Located under each armpit is a release point, its on the midline of each side of the body as high up under the armpit as you can get.

What you have to do is make like you have wings, elbows out to your sides and arms and hands parallel to the floor with your fingers extended across your chest with the forefinger against the rib cage.

Press gently on the points (it could be quite sore) with your thumbs and hold this position for a 10-15 minute meditation during which your mind should focus only on the sound your breath makes as you breathe.

If any thoughts arise, return to the breath after thanking the thought or emotion for coming to your awareness.

Initially, this should be done twice per day for 5-7 days, and after a rest period of a few days, repeated.

? Do not attempt to put thoughts or words around any experience you may have from this exercise - especially as the new born hadn't learned any by the time it was born.

? You can experience the effects of this release almost anywhere in your body - there may be burning sensations, freezing cold, an itch on the surface of the body or even just below the skin. If you are unsure of what you are experiencing, stop immediately.

WARNING

? **If you already have Heart problems of any sort, then you should not do this exercise without having your heart condition checked and continually monitored by a competent medical professional.**

? **As written, this is a Self-Help exercise. You should NOT, as a therapist (or for any other reason) attempt to do this release on another person. The therapy version to achieve this sort of release is VERY different.**

DIFFICULT WORDS MADE EASY

Ahimsa	**Ahimsa** is refraining from causing pain to any living creature. ...
Akshara	term for what can be roughly translated as alphabet. It refers to the basic units of sound. It derives its name from the fact that the first letter of this varnamala is 'a' and the last is 'ksha'. Combining these two characters one gets the term akshara which is used to denote the entire varnamala.
Alumpusa & start from Alampada their Nadi	The Alampurusa and Alampada Nadis anus, run up into the eyeballs, directing movement.
Amitabha Practice	The historical Buddha (Amitabh) Shakyamuni had disciples of many different capacities. Although he actually taught one single way to enlightenment, different parts of his teachings were taken as vehicles according to the capacities of his disciples. Basically, one can subdivide all of the Buddha's teachings into the two vehicles of 'Sutra' and 'Tantra'. '*Sutra*' is also called *"the causal vehicle,"* because one builds up the causes for enlightenment. In Tantra, *"the vehicle of*

fruition," one identifies with the fruit, or the different aspects of enlightenment.

To build up the causes for enlightenment means both to remove all causes for suffering and to practice the way which leads to the cessation of all suffering, to lasting happiness. In the Smaller Vehicle (Hinayana) the goal is liberation, because the illusion concerning a true self of the person together with all gross defilements is dissolved.

In the Greater Vehicle (Mahayana) the goal is full enlightenment. On the basis of the wish to liberate all sentient beings from suffering, even the subtlest veils of ignorance are removed and the state of highest wisdom, of complete omniscience, is obtained. This highest wisdom is nothing but the true nature of our mind.

If one has very strong confidence in the true nature of the mind one can directly identify with fruition itself, the different qualities of enlightenment. Based on the teachings about the Buddha nature which is present in all sentient beings, the Tantric methods of the Diamond Way bring about a very quick result.

It is said of the Diamond Way that the best practitioner can reach enlightenment within one single lifetime. This is extremely fast, especially when it is compared to the Sutra approach where enlightenment can be obtained only within aeons. But not every practitioner is able to use such powerful methods. Most traditions in the Mahayana are based on the Sutra approach. Only Tibetan Buddhism uses and transmits all the Tantric methods that the Buddha has given.

Amitayas	**Amitayas** Aparmita is the name given to Amitabha in his charter of bestrews of Longevity. Seated like Dhyana Mudra Buddha holding the vase, his special Emblem.
Amygdala	An almond-shaped neuro structure ... emotions in man. Usage: Many gestures reflect the **amygdala's** turmoil.
Anesthetist	An anesthetist is a highly trained medical doctor who after a six year medical training and two years of general hospital work spends a further five years undergoing special training and examinations before being registered to practise as a specialist in anesthesia.

The anesthetist's function is to make you insensitive to pain during surgery, to supervise your recovery from anesthesia, and to ensure you are comfortable afterwards.

Analogous	similar to and able to be compared with something else.
Anandamaya	Through creative vision, **Anandamaya** develops functional products that blur the lines between food and medicine taking the vision of health and well-being.
Angirasa	of mystical luminous race.

Animna These nerve currents are supposed to be filled with certain subtle juices which are referred to here as *animna,* very subtle exudation which controls the humors of the body.

Annamaya The first dimension is the material body, annamaya kosha. Anna means 'food', 'manifest matter', maya means 'full of'. There is no greater miracle than the human body. Although, scientifically, we look at the physical body as different systems which control the bodily functions, yoga says that these functions are nothing but manifestations of the interaction between energy and consciousness.

As we begin to experience the inner bodies, energy and consciousness manifest in a subtler form. So annamaya kosha is a dimension of existence in which we experience matter which is a combination of energy and consciousness.

Annasaya Annasaya is seated at the junction of drinking and eating.

Apana To exhale, downward energy, below the navel.

Asvini Muni Asvini.

Austere [adj] practicing great self-denial; "Be

systematically ascetic...do...something for no other reason than that you would rather not do it"- William James; "a desert nomad's austere life"; "a Spartan diet"; "a Spartan existence"

[adj] of a stern or strict bearing or demeanor; forbidding in aspect; "an austere expression"; "a stern face".

[adj] severely simple, "a stark interior".

Avatar — Re-incarnation.

Bardo — The word "Bardo" comes from the Tibetan words *"bar"* meaning "in between"; *"do"* meaning "island" or "marking point."

Also The period of Bardo is for 49 days. During the 49 Days after a being has died, we can pray for their auspicious rebirth. After that time period has passed, an image, usually a photograph, of them may be burned and offerings made.

This indicates that we free them from obligations in this life, and that we wish them well in their future existence.

The 49-day period is an intermediate, or *bardo,* state between existences.

Chhandogya Upanishad — That which is the subtle essence this whole world has for its soul. That is reality (truth). That is the soul. That you are,

Derangement — thrown into disorder, insanity.

Devadatta — Devadatta was a cousin of Sakyamuni Buddha. Their age must be about the same. They both were very smart and talented; therefore, they competed often on various occasions. It is said that they challenged each other to marry Yasodhara. As a result of the games, Sakyamuni won over Devadatta and married Yasodhara.

Devadatta was jealous of the Buddha's fame and position. He tried to take over the Buddha's Sangha. Once, he wounded the Buddha by pushing off a cliff a huge rock onto a trail where the Buddha was traveling. He also tried to murder Sakyamuni with an angry elephant. Devadatta disturbed the Buddha's Sangha by misguiding his disciples.

Chapter 12 of the *Lotus Sutra* reveals the relationship between Sakyamuni and Devadatta. Although Devadatta is infamous as an evil person, he will attain Buddhahood in the future because he has been Sakyamuni's teacher in his previous existence.

Dharmakaya — or "Truth" or "Reality body", by which the Buddha is of the nature of the essential Absolute Reality, or "emptiness" (Shunyata), so called because it is "empty" of all finite characteristics.

Dowager's hump	an abnormal curvature of the upper back with round shoulders and stooped posture caused especially by bone loss and anterior compression of the vertebrae in osteoporosis.
Endogenous	Derived or originating internally.
Endorphins	endogenous biomechanical substances implicated in the alleviation of pain, produced as a result of body stress.
Eons	Aeon An extremely long period of time.
Ephemeral	lasting only for a short time.
Exacerbates	make something this is already bad worse.
Extradition	Handing over a person accused or convicted of committing a crime in a foreign state to the legal authority of that state.
Exudation	discharge or to be discharged slowly and steadily.
Gandhari Nadi	The Gandhari Nadi climbs from the navel, adjusting with the seven great veins. It spreads around the throat and takes seat under the tongue.
Garbhodaka Ocean	abode of that Supreme Personality of

Godhead who is lying on the bottom Garbhodaka Ocean.

Garuda Purana — This is in the form of instructions to Garuda by Vishnu. This deals with astronomy, medicine, grammar, and with the structure and qualities of diamonds. This Purana is dear to Vaishnavites. The latter half of this Purana deals with life after death. The Hindus of north-India generally read this Purana while cremating the bodies of the dead.

This has origin of verses in given as a swan

given great importance to the Garuda. There are eight thousand this book. This book should be gift along with an image in gold of to get prosperity.

Gastrectomy — surgical removal of all or part of the stomach.

Grigara — helps the cleansing of the tongue and nostrils, and the functioning of coughing and sneezing.

Hallucinations — Apparent perception of an external object not actually present.

Heinous — utterly wicked.

Hippocampus — [n] a complex neural structure (shaped

	like a sea horse) consisting of gray matter and located on the floor of each lateral ventricle; intimately involved in motivation and emotion as part of the limbic system; has a central role in the formation of memories.
Hiranyagarbha	The Golden Embryo; the Spirit in the Dream-State.
Hu	A beej mantra.
Ida & Pingala Nadi	The Ida and Pingala Nadis start from the right and left toes, go up gradually in a scissors pattern parallel to the back bone, into the head, and then passing through the nostrils return to the anus.
Immanent	present within something.
Jalasaya	seated at the junction where water separates from intake of food.
Japa through Ida	japa beej mantra "yang" concentration on Ida Nadi.
Jivanmukti	Spiritual Liberation.
Kapha	Mucus.
Karma	`for every event that occurs, there will follow another event whose existence was caused by the first, and this second event

will be pleasant or unpleasant according as its cause was skillful or unskillful.' A skillful event is one that is not accompanied by craving, resistance or delusions; an unskillful event is one that is accompanied by any one of those things. (Events are not skillful in themselves, but are so called only in virtue of the mental events that occur with them.)

Therefore, the law of Karma teaches that responsibility for unskillful actions is born by the person who commits them.

Kashyap	... **Kashyap Muni** (son of Maharshi Mareechi) was also doing Tap with his wife Aditi for 1,000 divine years.
Kaushitaki Upanishad	Belongs to the Rig Veda family.
Kramamukti	Liberation by stages.
Krimibhojana	wherein he will exist as a worm who is eating the tail of another worm as that worm is eating his tail.
Kumbhaka	The duration of Puraka, (Exhale/out breath) Kumbhaka (retained breath) and Rechaka (Inhale/In breath).
Kundalini	... In human beings, Shakti, the feminine aspect is called **Kundalini**. This potential energy is said to rest at the base of the

	spinal cord.
Kurma	or the 'Koorm Avatar' is the second tortoise-incarnation avatar of Lord Vishnu.
Limbic	The Center of Emotions ... 2 - The paleopallium or intermediate (old mammalian) brain, comprising the structures of the **limbic** system. ...
Lunar Nadi	Ida is regarded as the **lunar nadi**, cool and nurturing by nature, and is said to control all mental processes and the more feminine aspects of our personality
Malasaya	Malasaya is seated in the junction where stool separates.
Manomaya	After pranamaya kosha, we come to manomaya kosha, the dimension of mental awareness. This mental dimension is composed of two qualities, manas and buddhi. Manas is the rational, linear, sequential, thoughtful mind. Buddhi is the quality of discrimination which comes after knowledge, after the removal or the absence of ignorance. The practices of pratyahara aim at realizing and discovering the nature of our manomaya kosha. Harmony of manomaya kosha has

to be attained by also balancing pranamaya kosha. We cannot say that manomaya is different to pranamaya, and pranamaya is different to annamaya; they are experiences and conditions of life which cannot be separated from each other. However, for our understanding and to define the sequence of our practice, yogis have defined the functions of annamaya, pranamaya and manomaya koshas separately.

Marichi Prajapati	A rishi, created by the Divine.
Neuropeptides	... Many neuropeptides are also hormones released by non-neuronal cells. ... Many neuropeptides are also hormones outside of the nervous system. ...
Nirmanakaya	or "Transformation" or "Emanation body", which is visible historical form of the Buddha. Nirmanokaya.
Niyama	Niyama (Observances or Disciplines or Devotion)

'Niyama', a Sanskrit, word mean rules or laws. These are the rules prescribed for personal observance. Like the five yamas, the niyamas are not exercises or actions to be simply studied.

They represent far more than an attitude. Compared with the

yamas, the niyamas are more intimate and personal. They refer to the attitude we adopt toward ourselves.

Sauca - The first niyama is sauca, cleanliness. Sauca has both an inner and an outer aspect. Outer cleanliness simply means keeping ourselves clean. Inner cleanliness has as much to do with the healthy, free functioning of our bodily organs as with the clarity of our mind. Practicing asanas or pranayama are essential means for attending to this inner sauca.

Samtosa - Another niyama is samtosa, modesty and the feeling of being content with what we have. To be at peace within and content with one's lifestyle. Literally the word means happiness. There are occasions we work hard to get something. We get very disappointed when we don't get it. Some people will get into extreme depression as a result. Some people may even contemplate suicide in extreme cases. We do these things because we do not have the discipline of being content with what we have. We should accept that there is a purpose for everything - yoga calls it karma. In 'Celestine Prophecy', James Redfield calls this synchronicity. The real meaning of samtosa is 'to accept what happens'. God has a plan. Christians prays, 'Thy will be done.' Accept what God has given us with humility and happiness. Be happy with what we have rather than being unhappy about what we don't have.

A commentary on the Yoga Sutra says: "Contentment counts for more than all sixteen heavens together." Instead of complaining about things that go wrong, we can accept what has happened and learn from them. Samtosa encompasses our mental activities such as study, our physical efforts, and even how we earn our living. It is about ourselves-what we have and how we feel about what God has given us. It is about our whole outlook on life. Do we look at a cup as half empty or as half full?

Tapas - Tapas refers to the activity of keeping the body fit or to confront and handle the inner urges without outer show. Literally it means to heat the body and, by so doing, to cleanse it. Behind the notion of tapas lies the idea that we can get rid of the rubbish in our body. Asanas and pranayama are tools we can use to keep ourselves healthy. Another form of tapas is paying attention to what we eat. Eating when we are not hungry is the opposite of tapas. Attention to body posture, attention to eating habits, attention to breathing patterns-these are all tapas that help to prevent the buildup of rubbish in the body, including excess weight and shortness of breath.

Tapas makes the whole body fit and well functioning. It gives us the discipline of developing healthy eating habits and prevent us from getting high cholesterol, high blood pressure and heart diseases.

Svadhyaya - The fourth niyama is svadhyaya. Sva means "self' or "belonging to me." Adhyaya means "inquiry" or "examination". The word svadhyaya literally means, "to get close to something." It means to get close to yourself, that is, to study yourself. It could also mean meditation or contemplation. It teaches us to be centered and non-reactive to the dualities, to burn out unwanted and destructive tendencies.

All learning, all reflection, all contact that helps you to learn more about yourself is svadhyaya. In the context of the niyama the term is often translated as "the study of ancient texts." Yes, yoga does instruct us to read the ancient texts because we cannot always just sit down and contemplate things. We need reference points. The world is changing fast around us. We can read the Bible or a book on spiritual healing or one that is of personal significance or the Yoga Sutra. According to the Yoga Sutra, as we progress in our self-examination, we will gradually find a link with the divine laws and with the prophets who revealed them. And since mantras are often recited for this purpose, we sometimes find svadhyaya translated as "the repetition of mantras."

Isvarapranidhana.

Isvarapranidhana means "to lay all your actions at the feet of God." It is the contemplation on God (Isvara) in order to become attuned to god and god's will.

We should accept the fact that we will not always get everything we want. Sometimes we get disappointed. Things do go wrong. This is the reason why samtosa (modesty) is so important. We have done our share. We have done the best we could under the circumstances. We can leave the rest to a higher power. In the context of the niyamas we can define Isvarapranidhana as the attitude of a person who usually offers the fruits of his or her action to God in daily prayer.

Orifice — an opening.

Paradigm — A typical example, pattern or

model of something. (2) A model underlying the theories and practice of a scientific model.

Parapsychology — Parapsychology is the scientific and scholarly study of certain unusual events associated with human experience. These experiences have been called "psychic" for want of a better term.

Please note: A common misconception is that a parapsychologist is a psychic. Not so. Likewise, a child psychiatrist is not a child! Instead, a parapsychologist is a scientist or scholar who is seriously interested in the "paranormal." Unfortunately, many telephone books and on-line sites use "parapsychologist" as a synonym for psychic entertainer, mentalist, conjurer, astrologer, or psychic reader. *This is an inappropriate use of the term "parapsychologist."*

P'howa — The practice that is done at the time of dying is called *phowa* or *powa* in Tibetan, meaning "transforming." That is, the consciousness is transformed by being ejected from the dying body, to be liberated and entually, received or transferred to another form of existence.

There are 4 ways to accomplish this transformation, through the Dharmakaya, the Sambhogakaya, the Nirmanakaya or through the forceful method known as *chetsab.*

P'howa Prayer	Through your blessing, grace, and guidance, through the power of the light that streams from you: May all my negative karma, destructive motions, obscurations, and blockages be purified and removed, May I know myself forgiven for all the harm I may have thought and done,May I accomplish this profound practice of *phowa*, and die a good and peaceful death, And through the triumph of my death, may I be able to benefit all other beings, living or dead.
Pitha	Bile.
Plotinus	Plotinus is considered to be the founder of Neo-Platonism. Taking his lead from his reading of Plato, Plotinus developed a complex spiritual cosmology involving three hypostases: the One, the Intelligence, and the Soul. It is from the productive unity of these three Beings that all existence emanates.

The principal of emanation is not simply causal, but also contemplative. In his system, Plotinus raises intellectual contemplation to the status of a productive principle; and it is by virtue of contemplation that all existents are said to be united as a single, all-pervasive reality.

In this sense, Plotinus is not a strict pantheist, yet his system does not permit the notion of *creatio ex nihilo* (creation out of nothingness). In addition to his cosmology, Plotinus also developed a unique theory of sense-perception and knowledge, based on the idea that the mind plays an active role in shaping or ordering the objects of its perception, rather than passively receiving the data of sense experience (in this sense, Plotinus may be said to have anticipated the phenomenological theories of Husserl).

Plotinus' doctrine that the soul is composed of a higher and a lower part -- the higher part being unchangeable and divine (and aloof from the lower part, yet providing the lower part with life), while the lower part is the seat of the personality (and hence the passions and vices) -- led him to neglect an ethics of the individual human being in favor of a mystical or esoteric doctrine of the soul's ascent to union with its higher part. The philosophy of Plotinus is represented in the complete collection of his treatises, collected and edited by his student Porphyry into six books of nine treatises each. For this reason they have come down to us under the title of the *Enneads*.

Pranamaya	The next layer of experience is anamaya kosha, movement of the pranic force directing our physical and mental activities. This movement happens through nadis or channels, conductors of energy which are controlled by the six chakras. Mooladhara chakra controls the elimination of accumulated toxins from the body and mind. In the physical

process, what we eat is eventually excreted, but while it is inside the body we derive nourishment and energy from it. In the same way there is also a process of elimination in the mind. However, we do not understand this process.

We tend to accumulate experiences in the form of the five kleshas, whether it is ignorance to begin with or the fear of death to end with. We do not eliminate them from the mind, but retain them in the form of experiences. Human consciousness revolves around those memories and experiences because of another factor which is the ego.

We have to learn how to eliminate things from the mind and retain tranquility and calmness. This can happen when we begin to work with our pranamaya kosha. To help in the understanding of inner release, we have to work with swadhisthana chakra, which represents the inner mind, the unconscious, the storehouse of experiences and memories. When memories plus experiences are stored in the inner mind, they are known as samskaras or impressions. Samskaras can be eliminated or transformed when we learn how to work with our pranamaya kosha at the level of swadhisthana chakra.

Dynamism of mind, aggression in our personality, whether physical, mental or emotional, is controlled by manipura chakra. When we work with manipura chakra, we transform the energies which are manifesting there at present to eventually experience the sattwic sate of being.

Anahata chakra controls the manifestation and projection of feelings and emotions. It deals with the qualities of attraction and repulsion in our nature. Vishuddhi chakra, behind the throat, is a centre through which we learn how to interact in the world efficiently, effectively and creatively. When we work with vishuddhi chakra, we change our outlook, our vision of life, and there is enhanced creativity, positivity and optimism coming out as improved communication.

The sixth chakra is ajna, the doorway between the manifest energy and consciousness and the unmanifest transcendental energy and consciousness. It allows us to move from the manifest dimension to the unmanifest aspects of our personality. All six chakras are dealt with when we are trying to manage pranamaya kosha.

Pranas — Air.

Prarrabda — Though the term is a philosophical jargon special to the theory of transmigration, we shall expatiate on its definition to get over the apparent bewilderment about it. After all, the idea that something called *prarabdha* forms the material of our life is perfectly in keeping with our strong claim for doership, i.e., *purushakara* (self-effort or self-enterprise). The theory reveals that from our previous births we carried forward some impressions, both good and bad, which have set in motion our present life. `It follows knowledge, work and past experience ' confirms the *Brihadaranyaka Upanishad.*[1] It is everybody's knowledge that a person's worldly business account ends in a *net* gain or a *net* loss. Whereas this karmic account varies from it in a peculiar way; it retains both good and bad entries. Everyone has to suffer her or his demerits or enjoy her or his merits.

Even the effects of good karma can be called `sin' as they lead to repeated births and deaths (*Apapaviddham* = *dharma-adharmadi-papa-varjitam;* Shankara). What we are today is the effect of our past karma. So the question of the future is open to us. It will be shaped by our present only. Between the future and the past there is a continuous change which is called the present. Present is nothing but an awareness of a *presence*.

For, this change presupposes an awareness of the presence (of the Self) of which we are unconscious. He who lives in the past is dead even as he who lives in the future is never born. A serious reckoning of the present (the *prarabdha)*, therefore, is the sign of sanity.

The scriptures are doubtless about the law of karma of which *prarabdha* is the dynamic part. It is said: *avashyameva bhoktavyam kritam karma shubhashubham*--one has to reap the fruits of one's actions, both virtuous and sinful; or *prarabdha-karmanam bhogadeva kshayah*--fructifying karmas are exhausted only by reaping the results; and when all the *prarabdhas* are destroyed, the manifested universe vanishes.[2] However, a reasonable understanding of the variety of *prarabdha* is necessary to gird up our loins against it.

Our own experience has helped us to classify *prarabdha* into three groups: *svechchha prarabdha* (what is produced by our desire to enjoy), *anichchha prarabdha* (what is produced unexpectedly) and *parechchha prarabdha* (what is produced through the desire of another). As we have already seen, God does not thrust them upon us.

***Svechchha prarabdha*:** It is not unfamiliar. It evokes in us the desire to enjoy life. We are enchanted by a spell of its apparent charm. No wise man is required to tell us that a major part of our suffering is caused by our unbridled hankering for enjoyment.

We suffer deliberately as we commit ourselves to harmful, risky or irresponsible activities. A patient under strict diet eats forbidden food; the result is obvious. Who is to blame? A thief steals and, if caught, suffers detention. Who is to blame? No act of dishonesty ever goes unpunished. If the act is acutely dishonest and harmful, an immediate punishment befalls. Instances around us are aplenty to prove the truth in it. What to speak of ordinary people, even the chosen ones, the men of wisdom, cannot escape such *prarabdha*. We get a big word of hope when the *Gita* (3.33) comments: Even a man of wisdom behaves according to his own nature. Beings follow their nature. What can restraint do?

In respect of instinctive actions, Shankara does not reckon any distinction between a jnani and the animals when he says: *pasvadibhishcha avisheshat* (Shankara's introduction to the

Brahma Sutras). It is normally beyond God's concern to do otherwise; because, if a person intentionally harms himself, what law can prevent him? As we are our best friends, so can we turn to be our worst enemies. Like moths we fly into roaring fire. What can restraint do unless it is imposed by ourselves?

Do we ever find time to cogitate how a larger part of our time is wasted unthinkingly under the sway of this *prarabdha*?

We do not reckon on this, because we don't feel anything abnormal about it. All our day-dreamings, building castles in air, are instances of this kind of *prarabdha*. It seems to be relentless. So it is indeed inexorable, say its advocates.

***Anichchha prarabdha*:** This is like getting things we have not even dreamt of. Unexpected receipt of anything comes under this group. We give vent to our ire for suffering only, whether it is expected or unexpected. But what happens if we unexpectedly get riches? A poor fellow digging a well may get jewels worth a fortune. Likewise many unexpected things happen in one's life.

The Ramayana says they are also due to one's *prarabdha*: that unsought for thing which we receive also comes under our *prarabdha*[3]. This again has been confirmed by the *Gita* (18.60) thus: O Arjuna, being bound by your own duty born of nature, you being helpless, you verily do that which you do not wish to do, owing to indiscrimination.

Our delusion or indiscrimination is that we are the doer, the agent. Then why don't we acknowledge this *prarabdha* as a product of our own nature? Because the sense of delusion is filled with pessimism. Is the theory of *prarabdha* so fatalistic? Well, the doubt is not unreasonable or unfounded. We shall try to find out the answer that the scriptures give shortly. For the present, let us proceed to the next group.

***Parechchha prarabdha*:** It means a *prarabdha* enjoyed or suffered by one through the desire of another. It is a third kind distinct from the earlier two groups. Let us rummage through our experience. A peculiar fact comes to light, that in the course of our life we, in spite of ourselves, get into a scrape. We do invite pleasures or pains as a consequence of our feelings for others or out of our personal and social obligations and responsibilities. It is called `fructifying karma through the desire of others'-- *parechchha prarabdha*.

Do we ever like to withdraw from such karma to avoid increasing our suffering? Let us remain thoughtful for a while and then say, 'No'. That means there is no way out of this problem! The question is, whcther we ourselves want it. We do not; rather we cannot avoid it. Because it is what life is all about. Swami Vivekananda very rightly observed, `They alone live who live for others.' It may amount to embracing death voluntarily. It is so, only in a noble sense. For, it does not imply a termination of life, once for all, but pledging of the whole life for others and in return suffering many death-throes while still alive. The fragrance of such a life wafts along to bring joy to many while the dedicated life itself, like an incense stick, gets burnt to ashes. Such people actually do not bother to burn all their desires for their own enjoyment and happiness. It is a *prarabdha* which is suffered by the doer and enjoyed by those they serve.

Precognitive	foreseeing the future second-sighted, clairvoyant prophetic, prophetical - foretelling events as if by supernatural intervention; "prophetic writings"; "prophetic powers"; "words that proved prophetic".
Psilocybin	a hallucinogenic compound obtained from a mushroom psilocin hallucinogen, hallucinogenic drug, psychedelic drug, psychodelic drug - a psychoactive drug that induces hallucinations or altered sensory experiences.
Purushottama	Highest being.
Rajas Guna	Rajas leads us to action, often with great expectations of particular kind of result or reward for fulfilment of one or the other of manifold desires. Most of the actions of ordinary people are tainted with desire of expectation. And as the saying goes, 'jahan hai aasha, vahii hai niraasha', being two sides of the same coin. He who expects too much is likely to be disappointed often.

In Rajas, it is this disappointment, failure of fulfillment of desires, failure of getting the desired results of actions and the greed that brings forth misery and unhappiness. It is thus not too good to live in Rajas for too long, and nor is dying in Rajas. It does not elevate the soul. It keeps you in the middle.

Sambanda	Relationship.
Sambhogakaya	Or "Complete Enjoyment body", by which the Buddha exists as a transcendent, eternal, celestial being; a primordial archetypal deity or Tathagata Buddha.
Sangini & Suhu Nadi	Guhu, Sangini and Alampada combine in 'kapha' creating widening of the eyes, deepening of the eye-socket, excessive sweating of face, and anxiety resulting in depression, deeper tamas.
Sattva Guna	Satva guna leads us to happiness and enjoyment, irrespective of the results of our action. It leads us to thoughtful Nishkama Karma. Here we do our work considering it as our laid down duty and we stop bothering about the results and keep no expectations. We face the situations of life calmly and as they present, keeping our inner peace and balance. Satva guNa is light and knowledge, wisdom and the calm and quiet of mind. Satva guNa elevates the soul. Dying while in Satva guNa, you are born in a celestial birth or as a saadhaka to elevate yourself further.

Slanchalasaya	Slanchalasaya is seated in the junction where urine separates.
Solar Nadi	Begins and ends to the right of sushumna.
Spatially	Having to do with space.
Sruti	That which is heard, and refers to the works of ancient, unknown poets and writers considered to be fully authoritative as Holy Scripture.
Stula	Coarse.
Subsist	maintain or support yourself at a basic level.
Subtle Body	so delicate or precise as to be difficult to analyze or subscribe.
Suklasaya	Suklasaya is seated in the junction where semen is stored.
Supernal	Being or coming from on high, heavenly, ethereal, located in or belonging to the sky.
Susumna Nadi	The Susumna Nadi appears at the bottom of the anus. It combines with Ida and pingala and with life air goes unto the top of head, sharing breaths.
Sutratma	The Antakarana is the thread that is

usually spoken of that the disciple creates through meditation, understanding, spiritual practices, and specific focalized spiritual work to create the thread, and later cord of energy. The disciple does receive help from the soul and later the monad in this process, however, the first half of the work must be done by the disciple.

The monad already has a thread or cord of energy that extends from it to the heart chakra of the disciple on earth. This cord of energy is called the sutratma, life thread, or silver cord. The soul has a thread or cord that extends from it to the pineal gland of the disciple which is called the consciousness thread. Knowledge utilizes the consciousness cord. Wisdom energy utilizes the Antakarana when it is built.

In Lemurian times the sutratma or silver cord was the principal cord in operation. In Atlantean times the consciousness cord became more activated. In this present Aryan age it is now to build the Antakarana and rainbow bridge and make it totally activated.

The Antakarana is like a spiritual filament of light that is built like a spider builds his web. This thread is spun by the disciple in life after life, and it is only that which is of a spiritual vibration that can energize it. The consciousness cord contains the mental qualities from the soul. The Antakarana is constructed of only spiritual/mental qualities from the soul.

The sutratma and consciousness cord have been constructed since man's first inception into the material world. The Antakarana has grown very slowly because a person has to step on the probationary path for this work to even begin.

The sutratma and consciousness cord work from above downward. The Antakarana works from below upwards. In the final stages of the building of this cord at the fifth initiation and ascension these three cords merge, integrate and blend together, just as the personality, soul, and later on, the monad merge. It is through the creation of the Antakarana that this whole process is allowed to take place.

Tamas — Tamas keeps us in a state of ignorance, sloth, laziness, inaction and darkness. Ignorance and inaction invariably bring about misery and unhappiness. As the saying goes, 'Ignorance of law is no excuse'. So a Tamasic person lives in total ignorance of spiritual laws and violates them knowingly or unknowingly and often brings himself to sad ends.

Not only living in Tamas is inappropriate and unhealthy, dying while Tamas is predominant in you is also fraught with grave danger of being born in lower yoniis or as insects and animals. How sad! It is certainly not proper therefore to lead a life in Tamas.

Tara — White Tara is an emanation of Tara who is

connected with longevity. One calls on her for health, strength, and longevity.

Her white colour indicates purity, but also indicates that she is Truth complete and undifferentiated.

She wears the Bodhisattva ornaments.

She has seven eyes: the two usual eyes, plus an eye in the centre of her forehead and eyes in her hands and feet. These indicate that she sees all suffering and all cries for help, even in the human world, even in the worlds of pain, using both ordinary and psychic or extraordinary means of perception. She carries day lotuses.

This Tara is also known as Samaya Tara, meaning Vow Tara. This refers to Tara's vow to save all beings and also to our vow, which is a Bodhisattva vow like Tara's.

Whereas the Green Tara is a young girl and has a mischievous or playful nature, the White Tara is represented as a mature woman, full-breasted and wise.

Some practitioners comment that the energy of the two Taras feels a little different.

Green Tara is very immediate and quick. One calls to her for immediate assistance, and also often for help with worldly things like lover, wealth and so on, as well as spiritual things. She feels very close.

White Tara seems to help more with longer-term problems, particularly problems of physical or mental health. It sometimes seems as if she is more distant, harder to contact at first. Then it is as if she sends us healing energies and mystical power and understandings.

Often one sees, in pictures of the Bodhisattva Avalokiteshvara (Tib: Chenrezigs), the two Taras in front of him - the White Tara to his right, and the Green to his left.

Similarly, Padmasambhava (Tib: Guru Rinpoche) is depicted with two of his consorts. The Indian princess Mandarava, with whom he accomplished[the Rainbow Body practice, is identified with White Tara.

The Tibetan princess Yeshes Tsogyal, his consort and a source of many important lineage teachings (for example the Kandro Nyin-thig), is identified with the Green Tara.

White Tara is Buddha family (some also consider her to be partly in Lotus family), whereas Green Tara is in the Action family and is the consort of Amorgasiddhi, the Buddha of that family. The practices of both are very important: White Tara is especially important in the Sakya teachings.

White Tara has her own mantra. It is: OM TARE TUTARE TURE MAMA AYURPUNYE JNANA PUTIN KURU SVAHA. (Ohm Tahray Totahray tooray mahmah ahyoopoonyay jahnah pooteen kooroo swah hah).

Temporal-Lobe — The temporal lobe is part of the cerebrum. It lies at the side of the brain, beneath the lateral or Sylvian fissure. The human

brain glove. The would	looks something like a boxing temporal lobe is where the thumb be.
Tenacious	Firmly holding onto something
Torpor	Apathy, dullness, a state of mental and motor inactivity with partial or total insensibility, extreme sluggishness or stagnation of function. Synonym - lethargy.
Udana	"As in the Great Ocean, O disciples, there is but one taste, the taste of salt, so O disciples, in the doctrine which I preach unto you, there is but one taste, the taste of Deliverance."
Usnishavijaya	Another long-life deity is Usnishavijaya who embodies the life force of the Buddha.
Uttama-purusha	Supreme being.
Vacuousness	Total absence of matter, vacuity emptiness - the state of containing nothing.
Vahni Bija Japa	Mang: Salutation to the region of Vahni with his ten qualities.
Vanaprastha	Retired life.
Variegated	Having discrete markings of different

	colors.
Vata	Air.
Vijnanamaya	From here we come to vijnanamaya kosha. Jnana means 'wisdom', 'knowledge'; the prefix vi is a confirmation of the intensity of knowledge which is derived not only from the experiences and memories which we have gained in this lifetime, but also in past lives. There is a storehouse of knowledge in every one of us, but we are not educated to experience that inner wisdom.

Vijnanamaya kosha has the aspects of chitta and ahamkara associated with it. Chitta means the ability to know, to become the observer of what is actually happening, to be able to live a reality and not speculate or fantasize about it. Ahamkara is the ego aspect, in the real not the gross sense, knowledge of 'I', becoming aware of the identity of the self. This understanding comes when we work with vijnanamaya kosha.

Once we have worked with and understood the identity of 'I', the identity of the self, which is manifest in the world in the third dimension and which experiences the pleasures and comforts, pains and sufferings of life, we move into the experience of anandamaya kosha, the dimension of bliss, happiness, wholeness, and contentment.

Vyana	That breath which operates, residing in all the joints of men's bodies, is called **VYANA.**
Yama	Lord Yama is the God of death in Hindu belief, and it is common to refer to death as 'The Call of Yama'.